Lucky's Flashbacks

BY ROGER L. WILLIAMS

Order this book online at www.trafford.com
or email orders@trafford.com

Most Trafford titles are also available at major online book retailers.

Print information available on the last page.

ISBN: 978-1-4251-2740-4 (sc)
ISBN: 978-1-6987-1639-8 (hc)

Illustrated by Roger L. Williams
Edited by Shirley Janke
Cover Design/Artwork by Roger L. Williams
Designed by Roger L. Williams
Photography by Roger L. Williams

Trafford rev. 01/23/2024

 www.trafford.com

North America & international
toll-free: 844-688-6899 (USA & Canada)
fax: 812 355 4082

To my two mothers.

Preface

Yes, my name is Lucky. I do hope that for this roller coaster ride, you have your seat belt on. Why? Just writing about myself I had to wear a seat belt. This story is not for the weak. Yes, there were secrets, secrets untold.

To you, the Reader I know...you know even now I daydream that I'm singing for 10,000 people, and I was singing my song to you. I still have my Apollo picture on the wall in a frame since 1984. I look at that and I remember the good times: when Freddy Jackson's first report came in, "You are my lady." He's from Harlem, too. I can still remember the RKO movie theater on 116th Street, and, 7th Avenue, and down the block was the Lowes Theater also. Let's not forget Brooklyn, the Fox Theater back in late 1955 and the '60s they had it going on. If I died today I could say I did sing on Broadway three times and the Apollo too. I didn't know I had all these talents in me. The secrets are behind my eyes...which one you think it is is up to you to decide. Sometimes we have to change with the world. Remember, we can't get off. Now just stick around and everything will change, I promise. Out of all of this I'm blessed. I'm lucky to still be here right now today. Let this be a good day for you and I hope when all else fails, look up to God. He will listen to you I know, because I talk to Him at night right before I go to sleep. I'm not too old to say my prayers and it makes me feel whole. How about you?

Foreword

As a young child of six I didn't know if I would see my tenth birthday It wasn't easy. I don't blame my mother. I do blame some of what went on my father. In my father's life it was all about him having a drink and him having all the women he could get.

I was hurt as soon as I was born. The hospital gave my mother the wrong baby at first. After about an hour, the nurse came in my room and told her she was breast feeding another woman's baby. So you see once I came out of my mother the doctor slapped my behind, that was my first hit. But, as I said before, I won't blame my mother I was never given up, or put in a home. My cousins and sister weren't with me in my young life. It seems, I had to grow up at seven years old. I had to be a man or die for not being a man at 7 years old.

Acknowledgement

THERE ARE ALWAYS MANY PEOPLE to thank when writing a book, too many for me to name all of them one by one. But I have to thank in particular rida and Sam from Harlem. They always gave me sound advice over the last 30 years and of course their friendships. Also James Moore of Ohio who has always been there as someone to encourage me. In addition I wish to thank Janet for being family and just being there for us. And, of course, my Carmen, my counsin for over 50 years, and was like a younger sister to me. And my friend john and his family in nj; they are my family also I love them very much.

And most of all to my great aunt Lil for always believing in me. I love her like a grandmother and she is still inspiring me at the age of 96.

*U*pon writing this story I look for God to give me strength not only to write, but to keep the faith, all the way. There is a point that Lucky is trying to come across: He is putting a skillful presentation for you the Reader to make his or her mind up over the story of my life! I'm trying to put my actions in you head, my soul, my frustrations...not the Reader, but myself. I want you the Reader to make up your mind about Lucky, his thoughts in your mind, or could you just block it out? The heart is something else we have yet to fully understand. This story is not for the weak. Do not feel sorry for Lucky, me. As anticipated, how Lucky handles his flashbacks in a step by step manner, right before your eyes, Lucky makes it happen. Lucky finds out how to walk the walk and talk the talk.

Lucky never looks back. It's about staying ahead of the game.

I hope by writing this...I hope in some way I can make someone know that there is hope for you, and there is room enough for you in it. If you the Reader want a part in it then let me, Lucky, now remember God loves you no matter what. I'm still here at 59, God bless, and let's not forget streetwise.

My name is Lucky. That is the name my mother gave me. I'm name after my father's brother Big Lucky. So in Brooklyn I was known as Baby Lucky, Baby Lucky can you go to the store. I used to dust all of my grandmother's little knick knacks. So after awhile I got real good at it. I was going to church with my grandmother and her two granddaughters at a Catholic church. I was proud going to church with them, but my grandmother could pass for white, or so maybe something else. Well, she taught me a few things while I was living there. She lived at 48 Monument

Walk, but then moved into a two bedroom at 9 Monument Walk. I was being called Baby lucky even when I first came home from Vietnam, but as I say, that was a learning lesson for me at a young age. You see my father didn't teach me anything, whatever I learned I learned on my own. By the time I was seven years old I had to decide to live. I choose to live, for better or worse. To live is something else, a good project.

The story of Lucky' his life is that you have a front row seat, from birth to teenager and, young adult to full grown man I've grown into.

An impulse or desire that is in conflict with my conscious image automatically from the pressure of my energy with which these impulses become part of my unconscious. In plain English a mode of adjustment to urges and desires. It is almost as if I could hypothesize with someone on my terms. Yes, I did develop a way to talk to someone with no problems, but as love form upon me I can not act. At least...in a human way. Let me move on.

While I was doing my tour of duty in Vietnam I went to Sydney, Australia in June of 1970 for a week, staying in a nice hotel. I didn't have to spend much money there. There were only two of us who went there from my company. I had a nice time there. Myself and a few other servicemen I met there, maybe six or eight of them, went to this night club on the Avenue. We were drinking, buying the girls who were with us at the club drinks as well. So then they stopped the music and asked if anyone wanted to come on stage to sing. The people at my table told me, "Go ahead, Lucky! You said you liked to sing!" At first I said no. Then I said OK, so I got up and went up to the stage. I asked the musicians whether they knew the song "Stormy Monday" . Yes, they did. So they started playing and I started singing, forgetting the words to the song as I was half drunk. So I went back to the table. After awhile they told me Lou Rowels was in the back laughing. I couldn't help but laugh too. Afterwards, wouldn't you know that Sydney, Australia has this fountain in the middle of a four way street and some guy poured soap powder in it, just like they do in New York Central Park down on 72nd Street.

I would like to talk about my father's family. His mother was born in St. Thomas. I found out from my father that his grandmother left Sweden, ran from there, because of slavery. My grandmother had a brother, his family or grand family, had coffee plantations there. Well that would make me rich, right? No way.

So now my grandmother was killed in her doorway on April 6th, one day before her 35th birthday, five months before I was born.

Grandma was knifed to death by a crazy woman that lived on the same floor. I'll go into this later. Her mother was part Native American and my other grandmother, well all I know is that she can cook up some good food, but for her and Tee Te (Spanish for aunt) my aunt, that is my father's sister. My father's mother had five children, two brown skinned and the other three could pass for Puerto Rican or white, my father's two brothers, one younger and the oyher older.

My mother met my father in a coffee shop on 7th Avenue, Uptown 7th Avenue or Lenox Avenue. He has this West Indian look, with good hair always kept short, a handsome guy. But all the women on my mother's side were as fine as wine.

My grandmother who was killed used to go horseback riding with one of her brothers in Central Park West. Everything was easy and slow. Food was cheaper, the movies too.

I just found out about the honors to the African American Union soldiers. It was in the early 1860s when they found themselves fighting against the Confederate army of Northern Virginia. The United States Colored Troops who served and were sacrificed in those terrible times, they fought and died in their first battle at Wilson's Wharf. Turning back the Confederate cavalry, they fought their way into North Carolina in December of 1863, to free as many as 3,000 slaves. It was the first battle in the entire Civil War to free slaves. Hearing about this is music to my ears. Of course we still have a long way to go.

Lucky was born to Loni and Mae at the City Hospital in Harlem, New York at 4:42 A.M. in 1948. They had a room on the forth floor on 112th Street, but before I continue, five months earlier this crazy woman knifed my grandmother to death in the doorway to her apartment there. As it was told to me, Auntie said, "Ma Me, Look out!" My grandmother had a two year old daughter named Amy standing right next to her. She was my Auntie Fray. Grandma had a six month old son named Lenny also. Aunt Millie sent for both of them, but after two weeks ma came back to Harlem where she and my father got married in a Catholic church on April 25th, 1948 in east Harlem. In the meantime Auntie Fray was still in the Midwest at this time. They often talked about the blood on them. My mother was five months pregnant with me when the murder happened. My grandmother lived at 135 West 115th Street. So now, a few months past and my mother gave birth to a 5 pound baby boy.

When Auntie found out she and Lenny came back and told Mae that he's mine, talking about me. Ma said I had a lot of hair all over my body. Ma was still in the room with Loni, when Loni pushed Mae down the stairs while she was carrying her baby after a few months.

Nine months later Ma had a girl She named her Lucy Kept. I was about a year old when my father threw me up in the air. He was showing off in front of his friends outside on the street, when he threw me up, but then dropped me on the concrete. (I am still, at the age of 58, living with neck problems from this.) Ma came running to get me and take me to see a doctor, but nothing was broken.

Lucky was Okay.

Ma told me my father was a pimp out there on Lenox Avenue, about 110th Street to 116th Street. He had his name on his undershorts. Ma said she was through with him about two months later.

My ma, Auntie, myself, and my cousin Lenny moved to Brooklyn, right by King County Hospital. By this time I was two, my sister was one year old, and Lenny was three. Auntie Fray found out that she was going to have another baby. My sister and I had cribs across from each other. I was told that aunt Lil from the BX came and took my sister because she was sick. Ma told us, my sister and me, that we used to throw our number 2 at each other. I hit Lenny in the face with a coke bottle. I didn't mean it.

So now my other cousin was born. Her name is G-e. I got so close to my aunt that you would have mistaken her for my mother. So after a few months passed it was 1952. Auntie Fray went with her two kids to stay with G-Gs father somewhere in Harlem. Iused to cry for her when she wasn't around.

Now Auntie and my mother, and the four of us got on the Greyhound bus and headed to Milwaukee, Wisconsin, the Midwest. Granddad had made Milwaukee his home a few years before. Ma told me that gramps told his two daughters to leave, the girls Lucy and G-G, and take the boys back to New York City. My mother and Auntie didn't have any skills that I know of.

My great aunt Lil told me about her mother, which would have been my great grandmother. She attended college at Shaw University in North Carolina in the 1880s. Her name was Mary trifton She started teaching by the time she was 18 years old. She taught Latin in a one room school. Her mother's name was Sara Patrick. This was Roper, North Carolina. My great grandmother died at the age of 36. My grandma was 12, my great aunt Lil was 13 and lived in the Bronx. So they all came up north, some to New York City, and some to Mt. Vernon, New York.

My great granddad got married again. His name was Papa Dee. He died driving the trolley car no 321 in Mt. Vernon, New York. He was 59 years old.

I remember one time I was staying with my father in Brooklyn on the South Portland Street. I ran away. This was at night. I think it was around 1 or 2 A.M. I was around eight years old, so I was scared to ring my Auntie's and Uncle's bell. So I fell asleep in the park. It was Mt. Morris Park. The police shown a bright light into my face. They woke me up and asked what I was doing there. My Auntie was across the street on Mt. Morris Parkway, I told them. I was so scared to go over there, so they took me over and I got in.

They told me never to do that again. I said, yes, but I was happy to see my Auntie and Uncle.

> **FLASHBACK:** There was this bar on 111th Street and Lenox Avenue. I guess it was the place to hang out back then. Anyway, my mother used to take me there. This bar was on the Uptown side. Ma would take me to the back where you could eat if you wanted to. Her friends used to play five records for a quarter. I would dance and dance. They used to give me some change for myself.

> **FLASHBACK:** My father and I used to stay with his younger brother. His name was Jay. My father was a cook on the 2nd shift.

One time my father worked real late. My Uncle raped me at his house, where my father had made me stay while he was looking for his own place. I was around four or five years old. My mother did not find out until the 1990s. Even then she was mad. My father took me back to my mother's that same year.

Ma was still living with Sonny at the Whitehall Hotel. Ma told me they were taking me to Sonny's sister's house, for her to watch me. It was on 129th Street and 8th Avenue. Well, his sister wasn't there. Her kids were there and were about ages 12 to 15 years old. There were four of them. They told me to go to the back room, made me take my clothes off, even my socks. They told me to stand in front of the babes crib where they tied my hand behind me to the crib, tied my lower legs together, and then tore up some old paper, putting it around my feet, and setting fire to it. They made me act like an Indian running up and down the room with no clothes on. I ran to the front door to get out of there, but they stopped me, so I went to the window where it was raining. I sat on the window sill. They left me alone. I was crying for my mother.

Lucky's Flashbacks
ROGER L. WILLIAMS

I was saying, "Ma, where are you? Ma, where are you?" It seems the more I cried the more it rained. Ma came and got me that morning. I didn't say anything. I was scared of what Sonny would do to my mother. Back at the Whitehall hotel, ma and I went to the store. I made her a little box to keep her stuff in. I made them with ice cream sticks. We came in and he broke and cut up her clothes too. Ma said, "Let's go!" Before we could get to the door Sonny came in looking mad. He hit my mother in the face for nothing. She didn't move, so he hit her again. She fell to the floor. Then this damn man kicked her. I started to cry for "MA!" I started crying real loud. He picked me up and threw me by the wall real hard. Then he left. He hurt my back. I was crying, not for me, but for my mother. I thought she would stop breathing.

It seemed like it was forever. If she didn't wake up I would have jumped out this window, but no, she woke up. She was bleeding from her face. I helped her wipe off the blood. She got up after he left and took me to the roof of this hotel Whitehall. She told me that she would throw me and herself off this roof, because she didn't want me to see that. She gave me a hug and a kiss, and said, "Lucky, I won't hurt you. I knew ma had everything to live for: she had two children and a sister, and a father in Milwaukee.

FLASHBACK: I know my mother had her angel with her, my grandmother. So after three or four months Sonny was still hitting her.

FLASHBACK: This is really very hard for me to write this. One night my mother and this damn man were at the bar drinking. This was on 111th Street and Lenox Avenue. He hit her in the face, and she fell off of the stool. Then he jumped on her stomach. No one helped her up. I still cry for my mother. I cry for my mother and for all women on whom a man had laid a hand.

Well, after that ma left him, Thank God she did. Ma took me to live with my father. He lived on 102nd Street. He had a room.

I didn't stay for long, maybe a month or so. My father and his girlfriend were both on drugs. I was seven years old. I was there by myself. I guess my father's girlfriend went to the store. Well, someone knocked on the door. It was the police. They took something. So when my father's girlfriend came in it was just a room. The police were gone. But when she found out that I had let the police in she went into the back room and took a wooden hanger and beat me with it until it broke.

Well, it left a big bloody scar on the side of my leg. I was crying and crying, "It hurts!" Well, my father comes in from work, sees me and the blood on me. I told him what had happened. He beat the hell out of her, right in front of me. Nobody took me to the doctor's.

The wound just closed up on its own. So now my father took me out to the Queens to stay with his sister. Te Te was her name. I always liked her anyway. She never had any children. She had a small apartment in the basement. She brought me a folding bed. I had to sleep by the door. My mother came in there, Tee had asked her to come so that she could kick her habit with drugs. Well, after a few days she slept with Tee. Ma got up in the middle of the night and left with her bathrobe on. She ran into the police. They gave her a ride to the subway. She went back to Harlem to see her sister.

Ma was sick. She needed some dope. My father's other sister who could pass for a white...I saw her bring in Navy men at night. She stayed in the living room. I went to school where I was in the fourth grade. I was a Crossing Guard. I had a white belt around me. I was only there for two months before school was out. So after school ended I was back in the Bronx.

FLASHBACK: I made it to ten or eleven years old. My Auntie had another son whose name was Wendell. So, meantime ma was going with this nice guy named Guy. He was a nice guy to my mother. So they had a place on 105th Street between West-end Avenue and Central Park West. I think

Uncle Freddy went to jail. This one day they were all out. A knock on the door, I opened it, and it was the police. They were there to put us out. They asked me where is my mother or father. I said they went to the store. I thought I'd better get Wendell dressed and myself. The baby was six months old. So I got dressed up. I had just enough money to go to the Bronx. If I stayed we'd be put in a home. I was glad I did that. I knew how to walk from our apartment to the train station on Lenox Avenue and 110th Street, Prospect Avenue and walked down.

FLASHBACK: My mother and Auntie got a big room on the first hotel floor, in the back. It was on 83rd Street around the corner from broadway father's other sister, the one with the Navy men, was living there also. Her name is Betty. So her daughter's father was white, about 52. He did not like me or my father. Well, ma and me and Auntie were waiting in the front of the hotel when my aunt Pat came out. She was with her two daughters. Well, my aunt Pat told her daughters not to speak to us. My mother didn't like her anyway.

It was told to me when my grandmother was killed, my mother needed a mother...like to talk to. My grandmother didn't like my mother. My two cousins A and B went to live with our grandmother before I got there. One night or evening I was coming into the lobby. My aunt's boyfriend pulled out a gun and pointed it at me So I went yelling to ma and Auntie. They called the police. I heard my father found out about what happened. He beat him down. His name is Sam. So the days passed. No friends down there. I was just sitting on the ground in front of the hotel when I noticed people coming out in a cab's limo and cars. I was making a little change for myself. I didn't stay out too late, making about $2.50+ to $3.00. Still, that was a lot of money for a eight or nine year old. So I did that for about two weeks and then I stopped. It was in the summer, so there was no school. My mother knew this lady of the night. She wanted someone to walk her dog, wash her windows, and wash her things. That was cool. As long as everybody kept their clothes I made about $6 or $7. I could go to the movies, which was right around the corner. So after a few months I had to go to stay with my grandmother. Now my two cousins were there, the same ones that had been told by their mother not to speak to me or my mother. I was named after my father's older brother. He is Big Lucky. I found out that my Uncle raped his daughter and was always beating up his wife. You know my father and his two brothers would drink and start fighting.

FLASHBACK: Auntie and Uncle Freddy were living in Harlem. Uncle was making a lot of money. They were living in the treasea Hotel on 125th Street and 7th Avenue. That was the hotel for the rich and Uncle Freddy asked Lenny to go out on a date with Red Fox's daughter. Lenny was around 15 then. I'm about 12 or 13 years old. I'm back up in the Bronx now. Auntie and Uncle Freddy moved to 736 Fox Street to a ground floor apartment. My older cousin T.J. Lived down the block at 712 Fox Street. She had her three children there.

FLASHBACK: When my older cousin T.J. would sleep for two or three days, most of the time, the kids had little to do, but that's when I used to take my three younger cousins Carmen, Billy and George over the bridge to the wood factory. There we would get some wood. We had a saw and we would build little tables. I showed them how to make things, draw maps of New York City, the subway lines, and the bus line if they were to get lost. We used to make small tables and paint them, and take them around the block and sell them for a few dollars. That was fun. It kept all of us out of trouble. I took them there three or four times a week in the summer.

FLASHBACK: So now I'm 14. Now I went to live with Auntie and Uncle at 604 St. Mary's Street in a two sided building. T.J., my cousin, lived on the other side of the building. Auntie Fray lived on the 5th floor walk up. Windows were in the back. We had a family dog named Blackie. He was a street dog. He would walk Uncle Fray to the subway station and come back home. My older cousin would put a note in the dog's collar asking for a few cigarettes. They could put it in his collar and bring it back.

FLASHBACK: I remember when Wendell was first born. Uncle would walk the floor with him. I could hear Auntie saying, "Freddy, come to bed!" He would stay up most of the night with that baby.

*U*ncle would come in with a whole lot of money and throw it all over the bed. He would have money from different places in the world, give me and Lenny that money and we would go downtown to exchange if for American money. Then we would go to 42nd Street, the old 42nd street. I went to make a record as it only cost $.50. Lenny would go and play those games where you win things. Then we would buy something to eat. Afterwards we would head uptown My Uncle would buy anything that Lenny and I wanted. Uncle Freddy was good to me and Lenny then. So downtown we went to 42nd Street That was the old 42nd Street where everything was for sale. You name it, there is a good chance that had it. But I always had fun down there. Uncle Freddy used to come with lots of money and he would throw it on the bed. Everyone used to count it. Sometimes he came in with nothing. All of the family liked him. Auntie and Uncle had

7 cars in their thirty year relationship. He was good for Auntie.

I was still 15 years old and heard that Mr. James Brown was coming to the Apollo Theater, so Uncle bought me a brown suit and brown hat with a matching brown cane. He gave me enough money to take a cab both ways. Boy did I have a good time. I had to be skipped to the 6th grade and just six months later I was moved into the 7th grade. Now I was in Junior High School. The school was or is on 141st Street and Brook Avenue.

I found out that ma and Auntie went to jail for drugs. They were downtown on West 10th Street in a ten story building. It was just for women I tried to go down there and called up to the windows in there Ma and Auntie! I love you very much...." Meanwhile my father had a nice apartment in the Park Slope area which was a nice area. He had a one bedroom, ground floor apartment. It was nice. Ma and Auntie got six months in there. So I was in boys high school in Brooklyn. I stayed out 57 days. My father talked about that even when he came to Milwaukee, bless him.

So ma and Auntie came out. They came to Lonies apartment and Uncle to' My mother thought she might try to be together with my father, but three days later my father was going to hit my mother so I picked up a large knife. I said to my father, "I will cut you all over your whole body, from head to toe!" Next morning we left for the Bronx.

Ma and I took a train back to the Bronx, Auntie and Uncle went to his mother's apartment on 123rd Street and Mt. Morris Parkway. Ma called her younger sister Amy. She lived in Queens, New York. I started training as a police cadet earning $30 a week, but after Three weeks I couldn't keep up. It was far too hard for me, so I had to quit. Amy got me a job in the First National City Bank on 90th and Park Avenue, New York. That job was nice. I would go out and collect all the checks in that area and bring them back to the bank, put them in the night mail box. Meantime I rented a room in Queens. I didn't know how to rent. I paid my aunt Amy's family, that was in the next building, $30 a week. Well, after a month I didn't pay my rent. So what else...I called my mother. She came out to help me move my things back to the Bronx for a while.

Amy called me to tell me about a new school that was in esopus N.Y. Right out of kingston N.Y. I was going back and forth up to Newburg 60 miles up the Huston River. The school hasn't been used in 28 years. It was an old school for boys, but now it is a prep school. It had ten classrooms, a big gym, and a mess hall. The mess hall s had some hard work to do. So across the road was a motel with a diner there. So, the State of New York paid for meals for us.

There were around 30 of us. Some of us got paid. I got $67 a week, if you went to school. We had to stay up there Monday through Friday. The weekend was our own. Sometimes I would go down to the city on the weekends. Our school name was Esopus Prep where we got our G.E.D.s. I also went to Newburg in Upstate New York with Lenny when his grandmother had died. I met Lenny's halfsister Grace. After a few days Lenny went back to the city. I stayed. So Grace and I started going together then. My school was about 20 miles from Newburg. After a month and a half I talked Grace into moving down to Brooklyn with me on South Portland Street, right off of Dekald Avenue. After another month she left to go back to Newburg. I gave up the room and returned to school. I about 16 going on 17 then. Our graduation was coming up. We all got our rings, in April of 1967, at the Roosevelt Hotel in downtown Manhattan. I, my mother, my great aunt Lil, and Grace were there.

The ceremony lasted about an hour. We went next door to a bar so that they could all get a drink. It was in that April of 1967 that I found out that Grace was pregnant by me.

FLASHBACK: When I was 14, Lenny was 15, and my female cousin kim all signed up to go to Washington D.C.. It was a spur of the moment thing and only cost us $2 each from the Police Athletic Club. We all made sandwiches for the trip. We got off the train in D.C and strangers handed us these big signs to carry for a demonstration. We didn't know what they were doing. There were 50-75 or more buses all over the place coming from all over the United States. I talked my two cousins into walking up the Washington Monument with me. I counted the step, there were 1,500. Lenny and I still remember that. We got down and found some seats to rest. Only an hour later Dr. Martin Luther King Jr. stepped up to the podium to speak. And when he got up to the microphone everyone stood up and clapped for about 15 minutes. We were all the way back on the Mall, not realizing how important this man was or this day. It was just our day out of the Bronx, but we became part of history. It was August 1963 on a very hot day. That was his "I have a dream" speech

FLASHBACK: Around the same time, while living on Fox Street, there were three older sisters living there, that is, older than I was at 15. One of the sisters liked me. She brought me a winter coat, socks and underwear. The building was a two sided building. Anyway, ma found out about it and told me to give them damn clothes back. Ma went and told her that I was underage. So that was that. She told me to stay away, which I did. That following year, 1964, ma met a man named Guy. He was nice to my mother. He wore a brown suit, was about 58. Mr. Guy was a hustler, but not like Uncle Freddy who would steal 100 cartons of cigarettes. Guy and ma asked me if I wanted to sell the Sunday Daily News. You would get a free Superman comic book. I liked that no one would brother me. This was on 119th Street and 7th Avenue. I was there for three to four hours. Guy would come and pick me up in his car.

So after about three weeks of selling papers the paper, Guy and ma asked if I wanted to work in a store. I said, "Yes, yes!" It was a food store. He had his cousin in the back making sandwiches. I would ring up the items for the people. This store was on 114th Street, right off of 8th Avenue. I was making maybe $20-$24 a week. After two months Mr. Guy said he wanted to close up. So that was that. But within another month Mr. Guy had opened another store. This one would be on 8th Avenue between 113rd and 114th Streets.

So Lenny came down and got a job making ices out front. One day Lenny asked me to cover for him. He wanted to talk to a young lady. So I went and got the ice pick and started picking the ice. I put my right hand in there because I am left handed. When I pulled my left hand up my right hand came up. I had the ice pick right between two index fingers. Lenny went to get Mr. Guy. They took me to the hospital where they pulled it out. It didn't hurt because they gave me a shot. I hate needles. I told Lenny to do his own ices from now on.

FLASHBACK: In 1984 I had won two tickets to Fats Waller musical Aint misbehaving My cousin Carmen had come up from Florida at the right time. I took her to it. It was down-town. We had a nice time.

Now in 1985 I had won two tickets to Studio 54, which was just the hottest club anywhere. Carmen was in New York at the same time. Sometimes I think we have ESP. No joke! It was a party for some rapper's, but after a few hours a fight started. I told Carmen, let's go and we did. That same club was studio for the game show Password.

I used to always participate in contests, particularly when I was in prep school in Upstate New York. I used to write channel 11 WPIX TV. Back then they had a dance show called the Clay Cole Show. It was something like Soul Train or American Bandstand. So they wrote me back saying I could come there any Tuesday or Thursday. That was when the shows were being taped for later in the week. I made the show four times. It was 1967 that was a very good year. I always liked to be around show business people.

That same year I had a small record player and some 45s too. So I went out and bought a small can of good paint. I painted my record player gold and went out and bought an 8 x 10" frame. I painted my record gold and put it in the frame and told my friends I had a gold record. They said what is the name of the record? I said I don't know. I was told that my grandmother was mother and one of her brothers would go horseback riding in central Park. I'm slowly learning about my mother's father, my granddad, that he was a tap dancer and played the drums and sang. That goes to show you you are never too old to learn something new.

FLASHBACK: I was eight or nine years old when my mother almost died. She had what's called lock jaw, that is from using a dirty needle. I was staying with Auntie and Uncle Freddy on 85th Street between West End and riverside Drive. It was a quite and clean block. Well I just know ma will make it. When you get that the doctor has to make a very small cut in the jaw just below her neck. My father came over and told Auntie that he heard that mother was dead. Not true. "As the sky is blue, I'll come back to you Lucky."

FLASHBACK: So now we jump to when I was 17 years old. My mother had an apartment in the Bronx on Powers Ave floor. It was nice, so the lady that I've been seeing had a baby boy. His name is Van and while there my mother and I met a young white girl who had a son about a year old. We all became friends. My sone's mother is Grace. She brought the baby down. Myself and my son were baptized by Father Moore, September 1st, 1968. So now it is September 5th and I am leaving to go into the army. I kissed Grace and my son goodbye, and mother. I told her not to worry about me. So Grace and my son left to go back home to Newburg, N.Y. I had to go to Brooklyn to Fort Hamilton way down in Brooklyn Then I was sent to Ft. Jackson, South Carolina for eight weeks It was very hard the first four weeks, but I got through it. After eight weeks I was sent to another base in St. Louis. Now it was no more being nice! It was stand up tall, chest out. They wanted our boots to shine and shine and shine. That was for advanced training for another eight weeks. It was November of the same year 1968. We were in North Carolina to learn to build a bridge and tear them down. I liked that. First a rope bridge and then a steel one, and last a wooden one a week before receiving our orders was put up, and I found out I was going to Germany. So we all went home for Christmas in 1968. By this time my mother had another friend, his name was John. My mother moved in with him on 118th Street and 7th Avenue into a seven room railroad apartment. It was nice I guess. I went downtown and got myself a job with Macy's Department Store on 34th Street. I would stack all of the men's things, then put them up in the glass display case. I met someone there and we are still friends today. So after about one and a half months there I left to go to Lord and Taylors Department Store on 5th Avenue. That was a high price store.

FLASHBACK: I was at this store for about two months. I was doing good there doing the same thing there also. Meanwhile my sister Lucy came to New York. I finally met my sister. Both of us did not remember when we were together and little kids in Brooklyn. Lucy came down to my job to have lunch together. It sure was nice. She was pretty and now 17, and I was 18 years old. Well after about three and a half months things did not work out as far as Lucy living with us. So her boyfriend then drove up from Milwaukee to New York and came and took her back to Milwaukee. I heard ma crying. I know she felt real bad about that.

FLASHBACK: By now I had let my hair grow out and wore nice clothes It was April of 1969. On this one day I felt someone watching me. It was on a Monday, I know, because on Tuesday we had payday. Two white guys came in and asked

To tell you the truth, I had forgotten about the army.

They put me in handcuffs. My boss and coworkers said, "Lucky, you was in the service?" I said yes. I asked the F.B.I. guy to put my raincoat over my cuffs so no one could see them.

It was April 24th, 1969.

From there they took my down to some precinct downtown. They took everything in my pants and I spent the night there The next day they took me to Ft. DicksThis was like a dream or something. I couldn't believe what I was into. There were guards standing at their posts and holding guns, always watching all of us. They searched us going into the Mess Hall and coming out. One time, after about a month, they put this one Private guy into what they called the box: it was about four feet high and had a little window. So everyone started burning their beds, and everything. Now it was a riot! The TV news WABC News covered it and had that it lasted about eight to ten hours that day. I was thinking about my mother. She didn't know where I was. We were in South Jersey, about a three to four hour drive away. So finally my mother and Grace's father came to see me. I told ma not to worry about me. I'll make it no matter what. Right before she left ma threw me a half a pack of Kool cigarettes. Man I was happy, happy! You see if you smoked in there you had to smoke Pall Mall cigarettes, so 5 of us smoked one cigarette. There was really nothing else to do there. So after one and a half months I was taken to the airport to go to North Carolina. You see, down there you could smoke your own cigarettes, and buy your own writing paper, and candy.

FLASHBACK: Now again after about four weeks they posted everyone's orders. I wanted to see where I was going and they had me down for Vietnam. Damn! So we all had a week off. Ma was still living down in Harlem on 118th

Street in a fifth floor walkup. When I got back to New York I told mother where I was going. Ma said I didn't have to go, but I said I don't mess with Uncle Sam.

FLASHBACK: My first cousin Lenny went into the service a year before me. That is what ma told me. So Lenny was on his way home from Vietnam. I didn't see him when I came home on that trip.

I also told my son's mother that I was going overseas. It was very hard to say goodbye to ma, Auntie and Uncle. They were living up in the Bronx. So it came to pass that I was getting ready to leave, going to the 116th Street train station. Ma walked with me. She started to cry. I said don't worry ma, I'll write to you and Grace and my father Loni I had to go to the J.F.K. Airport. From there we flew to the west coast. There I got on another plane. So I was on my way half way around the world to South east Asia. I didn't know what to look for when we landed in Japan to fuel up. After that we landed in Vietnam. I was very nervous, that first day there. I had to get into a fox hole and stay there until it was clear, because there were rockets coming down near the airport.

FLASHBACK: After everyone got their orders where to look up your unit, some guy came up to me and asked if I wanted a cig. No, I said. I have my own. But this was a "cig" as we know it in New York City, so I took one. He said, No man, this is a reefer. Don't smoke the whole thing. I said, I'm from New York. It won't bother me, and smoked the whole joint. Next thing I knew I woke up 300- 5000 meters away. The Sargent tapped me and asked me where did I belong? I answered, with the 101st Airborne 319th Field Artillery. Someone drove me in a jeep to my unit. Then I thought, if I am going to die I want to go out high on a high note.

FLASHBACK: Now that I'm in my unit, the 319th Field

Artillery. Vietnam was scary. The mortars and rockets falling over us and our shelling of the enemy: "FIRE IN THE HOLE!" Happened so many times and I often didn't have time to cover my ears. I didn't see people dying from there, but I did see them getting shot at. I don't like talking about this and I don't go to movies about wars, even now.

FLASHBACK: I forgot to talk about when I was in cooking school for months and switched to baking school. It was fun what we cooked or baked. We would try each others food or cake. That was easy for me as my father was a cook and baker. So at the end of two months all 30 of us had a written test that really was hard. My teacher was a sargent. He said that he was getting ready to retire so he gave us all the answers for the test. No one said a word about it, although some of the guys didn't care if they passed or not. They were just getting behind...so that was that.

FLASHBACK: Back to Vietnam: I was a trained cook and baker, and a trained combat engineer. I remember one time we were flying out to my unit on the hill. I was bringing hot and cold food for about 25-30 men. We all had to eat. Sometimes we couldn't take our boots off for three or four days, because of rockets being fired on my company. I stayed in the fox hole for eight hours one time, and it rained for eight days straight. There was once when rats were in the and mongooses in the fox holes with us. There I was in the middle of a damn war. For what?! I had said this before one of my cooks got killed fooling around. He was on pills (uppers) and had come in from another unit. He was not paying attention, a white man who had not been there even two months, with mortars falling around him. Mortars fall without making a noise so they just land on you or not, depending on your luck and good sense. He didn't protect himself and ended up dead.

A lot of the guys were fighting for two to three days and nights. They were coming back to the company and I could see it in their faces that they were tired. So I made them some coffee, iced tea, and put on steaks and eggs. I also made a sheet cake. I always liked baking, because that was easy for me. I was called to Headquarteres It was guarded like Fort Knox or something. We never ate at night, only in the daylight as the Mess Hall was halfway underground. We slept underground.

FLASHBACK: I didn't go too far at any time. One time I almost died: we were pulling out of our unit with about four jeeps and two trucks. My truck was the last one because it carried all the food supply and stoves. A rocket landed near our truck. I told the driver to step on it! I think what saved my life was that not only my mother wrote from home, but my son's mother as well. And the white girl I met the night before I went into the army wrote to me: 3- 4 pages of love. She said that she loved me.

FLASHBACK; I was sent back to Headquarters again to be a night baker. This was for two and a half months. I would go into the underground Mess Hall at midnight and all I did was bake: pies, cakes, apple turnovers, etc. Sometimes a few guys would stop by and ask if I could bake them a small cake or have a piece of pie. They would bring me some beer. It was Old Milwaukee beer. I slept most of the day. I had a four band radio.

FLASHBACK: Once I was on Tower Guard Duty. I had my two way radio and a small flashlight. The tower was three stories high. There were four guards to my left and four guards to my right. It was around 2 A.M. They radioed in that they heard movement in front of the barbed wire fence down in front of the guys in the fox hole So I radioed in to...Fire! Fire! Fire! At will! No one moved, but waited until daybreak. Only then did we discover that there was a pig stuck in the fence. That pig was not fit to eat: he had too much lead in him. All of us were glad that it was just a pig, but that pig had about 10-20 holes in it. Being as I was the cook I had the power to make those guys clean everything, sometimes two times if I had a bad night. You see, nobody slept too hard. My Mess sargent didn't like me and I didn't like him. So now I was an E-4 and due to come home November 11th. Everybody over there always counted the days to going home, to the world that we knew. I was no different.

FLASHBACK: On November 5th, 1970 I was working in the underground Mess Hall with a foot of water there. I had been overseas for one year. The guy came and gave me and my roommate orders. I was going home four days early, on November 6th, 1970. I was so happy that I left my small four band radio and Jimmy Smith album. Boy was I happy! So about four of us were leaving Vietnam at the same time.

What really saved my life was that I had been made a cook and baker I couldn't have been safer most of the time as I worked in the underground Mess Hall for "Fort Knox" known as Headquarters.

FLASHBACK: After we packed up I just left everything. We bought some wine before everyone was going their own way. We got drunk and slept in a church. We woke up four hours later and the priest just said to clean up our mess. Then we all said goodbye to each other. I couldn't believe I was going back to the world on TWA. We stopped in Japan for fuel, then got back on and landed at J.F.K. I had picked something up in Japan for my grandmother. I found out that she had moved.

FLASHBACK: My grandmother adopted a baby girl. She

was about ten or twelve when I returned from Vietnam. Grandma was now old, but she was glad to see me. She moved way out in Brooklyn. I spent the night. I got up and kissed grandma goodbye, then got back on the train to Harlem's 118th Street where my mother was living. I made it there and rang the bell. Boy was ma happy to see me! She cried and smiled for days. I think she got in touch with Auntie Fraye who was living in the Bronx.

So I was really home at last at last. My mother's male friend Johnny was a limo driver. The next day, November 7th, 1970, I asked Johnny to drive me up to 125th Street. There was a music store there between Lenox and 5th Avenue. I bought a three piece red drum set and two cymbals that the man threw in another drum. So we came back. I couldn't wait to set them up.

FLASHBACK: I called aunt Lil in the Bronx. She was glad that I was home. In a few days I was up to see my Auntie Fray and Uncle Freddy in the Bronx.

Now back to downtown. Johnny gave me the last small room in the back.

FLASHBACK: When I was AWOL from the army after my sister left Grace and her brother came down from Newburg to see me that was the last time that we slept together in the middle room.

FLASHBACK: When I was in Vietnam, January 1970, my mother wrote me to say Grace had a baby girl named Cherry. I got really uptight. I had to take something to calm me down. Then I counted the months that we had slept together since April, yes, she is my daughter. Both kids in the same month two years apart.

$\mathcal{G}$etting back to me, Lucky, there I was playing my drums, teaching myself how to play the drums. These young ladies were eyeing me out from next door. I would say hello and that was that. Now after about a month I was doing well with my drums.

My mother went to the Midwest to visit family and I had lunch with my priest downtown. He dropped me off in front of my building afterwards. I ran up to the 5th floor as I still had a lot of energy When I got there the door was cracked open, even though we had a police lock on it. I ran to the back too, but my drum set was gone. Where we lived it was like Wisconsin Avenue in Milwaukee, Wisconsin. Something as big as that drum set you can't hide. It was talked about by the people on the 2nd floor. The lady there didn't like my mother and me. I didn't even know them. She had her four grandchildren and her grown son and daughter. I got mad as hell but at the same time ma was in Milwaukee and Johnny wasn't home so I couldn't prove that they broke into the apartment and took my drums.

I now was really mad at the world, but I started making friends with the young girls next door. They were sisters. Johnny kept bugging me about more money for that real small room, so I moved out. I moved into the YMCA on 135th Street at last no one to bother me Ma returned and I was still going down to see her. Sometimes I would sit on the steps and watch all of the girls walk by. Now I met another female. She said she lived down 112th Street in a room there and that she had a little boy. Her name was Windy. And while I was still at the YMCA I was reading the paper for actors and singers wanting notices. Someone told me that they were reading parts for a play in the basement there so I went there and read for them. I got the part. The play was Big Time Buck White and it was now the summer of 1972. I was 24 years old.

FLASHBACK: Windy and I got close. I was also keeping in touch with Grace up in Newburg. Windy's cousin was moving out of her apt on 7th Avenue between 134th Street and 135th Street. We moved into it, more like taking it over. There was no bed for Windy's son. His name was Vic. Johnny, my mother's friend, gave us some really big pillows to make a bed for him.

Now, some of the guys would come over to go over some of the lines from the play. I could tell Windy was getting tired and mad. My friends in the play had to stop coming over.

In 1971 I had gotten a job in the post office: Brooklyn nameB.A.T. I was a porter. This was before they had guards there.

FLASHBACK: Windy and I took the bus to Milwaukee to see my sister, grandma and my other cousin G g. We stayed a week. Mother was watching Vic. Windy and I didn't say a thing to each other on the ride home.

The play didn't go anywhere like I thought, but I made friends with one guy from the Black Paper, James Moore from Ohio. We still are friends today.

FLASHBACK: March 1972 going into April Windy and her son and I went down to meet my mother on 118th Street. They were shouting out loud to each other when the next thing I know Johnny pulled out a 22 gun and shot my mother in the leg and in the arm. Ma passed out. The boy was crying. I had Johnny by his legs getting ready to throw him out that fifth floor back window. He was around 120 lbs. My girlfriend said, "Lucky, your mother just passed out." She asked me to bring him in...so I did. I said, "Throw that damn gun out the back window!" We went to the hospital with her. They got the one bullet out, but not the other one. Ma came to stay with us for awhile. Then ma found a small apartment in the Bronx. It was on 141th Street between St. Anns and Brook Avenue on the second floor. My other great aunt from Queens gave her something to sleep on, a bed, that's all. Windy and I broke up so I stayed with ma for awhile. I had to sleep on the floor. That was cool.

Moving on I met a woman ma knew named Mary, a bar maid. She used to come by to see ma off and on. One day we hit it off so I told ma. She said, "Mary is married and her husband is 6' 4"." So I backed out of that.

Ma didn't stay there for more than two months. She found another apartment on Longwood Avenue in the Bronx in a fifth floor walkup. It was a nice size. Ma said that my sister was coming to New York from Milwaukee. Meanwhile ma went back to school to get her GED and got a job with the City of New York down in lower Broadway across from 26 Federal Plaza. I was proud of ma. I knew she could do it. She worked with about ten people. Ma always got along with people.

There was another young lady from ma's job. We got together every now and then. Ma brought a bedroom set and a sleeper for the living room. I went and got some wood and made a bar. It was black and red. Ma had bought two tickets to see Miss Lena Horn on Broadway. Ma took her daughter to the show. You see everybody has class, it just has to come out.

And in the same week I won two tickets to the dance party. I still have a picture of us dancing. This was 1974. We had a good time. At least I did. I was 26 years old.

FLASHBACK: So moving on, I made friends with the young lady that lived next door down on 118th Street. Her name was Dawn. I entered us into a dance contest to dance for 12 hours straight in the window of a record store on 241st Street, White Plains Road, the BX. There were four other couples; from Brooklyn, Queens, New Jersey, and Manhattan. We had the Bronx sewed up. Remember, I was 28 years old by now. So we were in that window and a lot of people stopped to look at us After 11 ½ hours you could see that we both were tired, but we kept on dancing. The police were going to give us a ticket because a lot of people stopped to watch us.

So we called WLIB Radio. They told us to go outside, so we did. The club the Bump was out, because we found out everyone hung out there. So we all had to go to this club on 125th Street, a nice big place. It was owned by Melba Moore's husband. That's when I found out that I was the oldest one there at 28. So ma came down. She just got out of the hospital. My X-girlfriend was there and present girlfriend. The people there passed around fried chicken at all the tables. So this is what a Best Dance Contest was like. Just before they called me Lucky and Dawn ma got sick from eating that chicken. So I caught her a cab. Right after that they called our names, "Lucky and Dawn from the Bronx!"

There we were where everyone was watching. I didn't care. I said to Dawn, "Let's do this!" I had a checked plaid suit and a pipe. So we did the Bop. At the end they said we all did so well they gave all five couples $100. That was cool. I got change for a $20 bill and gave Dawn her $50. I left afterwards, because she was in some guy's face that was a singer, and I went home to the Bronx.

My father was sitting there when I got back and said, "Well son, are you going to take care of me?" I said, "What?" And gave him a few dollars. I knew he wanted a drink. Ma was laying down. I went into her bedroom and said, "Ma, you feeling any better?" She answered, "A little Lucky." I gave her $20. Dawn and I were still friends. After about six months ma said that she had found another apartment downtown in Central Park West on 108th Street. It was small, but nice. Ma was still working in lower Manhattan across from 26 Federal Plaza. And so it came to pass that ma moved down to Central Park West.

I had gotten an apartment on 170th Street in the Bronx. It was a one bedroom. I took the bar that I had made for ma, lowered it, and made a chain lamp. Then I got a high riser for the living room, but no bedroom set. It was on the fourth floor. My apartment windows were in the front of the building. This was in 1977.

After living there for two months with my uncle Ted staying

there on and off, ...

FLASHBACK: Since my bedroom was empty a friend of a friend asked if he could rent the room from me. I said okay. His name was Lue. Now he brought this long record player. You know it opened in the middle and had an AM/FM radio in it. So I said that the rent would be $100 a month. But his record player was too big for the bedroom. I had a small record player. I told him to put his in the living room and put mine in your bedroom. He said fine. So in his room he had a bed that was on the floor and a straw chair. So now a month came and went, but no rent money. I knew something wasn't right. When he and his girlfriend were home they would go into the bathroom for long periods of time: she was on his shoulders.

When he was out I looked in all the closets. I found a set of works, that's a needle, and a cooker to burn and cook it. He is on drugs. He was using dope. This guy was shooting up right under my nose. So I put the stuff on top of the bar. My uncle was there and we waited until he came in. I asked him, "What the hell is this shit!" Then he said, "Why was I going into his closet?" I told him, don't want anyone around me that is using drugs." So I said, "Where's my rent money?" He didn't have it. So I said, "You've got 15 minutes to get your stuff out of here!" He asked me, "Well, what about my bed and record player?" I said, "That's mine." My uncle told him, "You can go out this window or you can go out the door!" He left, came back with a friend and some bags. And I told him, "Don't let me catch you in the street!"

A female came to see me. She used to go with one of my cousins. We got some beer. Next thing we had our clothes off making love on the floor. She wanted to have a baby by me. It didn't happen. We were almost drunk. We were sitting on the floor and she wanted to make out with me. I said okay, so we did. She knew all of my family.

Moving on, it was in the 70s when my sister came to New

York. Great uncle was Upstate in jail. He told me when my sister was in town to bring her by to see him. That is my grandmother's brother. We got up there late and had maybe a half an hour visit. And I had brought all of this chicken. They talked while I ate the chicken. I was glad to take my sister up to see him. He always said that he loved both of us.

> **FLASHBACK:** I still remember Kelly Street 811, the corner building with five floors. So back to the apartment in the Bronx. There I moved out. I just took the straw chair and broke up the bar that I had made for ma. I stayed with ma for a few days until I found a room on 122nd Street, Harlem. It was $16 a week for a small room, but it was mine.

Ma had made some friends on Central Park West. She wasn't too far from Auntie, about four or five blocks on the Park Side. Ma made friends with a guy next door to her. He said he had a black and white 25" TV that I could have if I wanted. By then I had moved to Riverside Drive to a real nice place overlooking the river and looking out to New Jersey. So, yes, I got that TV. It was big. I took a cab and had someone to help me bring it to my room. Three months later I moved out. I brought the TV back, but when I got out of the cab the cab driver broke the set. Well, that was that.

It was 1980 in the winter and time to put on coats. I didn't have a job and wasn't going to sit around much. I went down to Jacksonville, Florida to see Carmen and her two sons ages ten and five. I was going back and forth, gaining weight at the same time. I stayed down there for awhile. Ma was working in Queens and sending $50 a week for about six weeks. I still didn't want to live there.

Carmen's girlfriends used to come over and one of them started talking to me. We became a couple for awhile. She had two young kids and a husband that didn't care for her anymore, so she packed up and went to her mother's place in another state. She used to write to me, once I got back to New York.

By now it was 1983 and I was 35. I had a friend who knew someone who could take a picture of me for modeling or acting. So there I was standing with one leg on a bench and sitting down. Over all they all came out nicely; nine pictures of 8x10s for $35. Yes, I know it was cheap. I had wanted to be on the soap All My Children and I was trying to start my own fan club. To this day I do not know who I gave my pictures to.

There was a friend of mine who also wanted to be on TV. He had his pictures as well. He was sitting in a bar with his back to the door when someone shot him in the back of the head. They had been looking for his brother. That bar was on 112nd Street and St. Nichols Avenue. I felt real bad about what happened, particularly as it they had found the wrong man. Later I heard that they found his brother as well.

> **FLASHBACK:** While ma lived on Central Park West, Auntie was living about four blocks away. I would always go and see them both. Auntie Fray was living on 110th Street on Lenox Avenue. By now I was doing any kind of work I could find, whether on or off the books.

> **FLASHBACK:** Carmen would come down to the city, Van, my son, was twelve and Cherry was just ten years old. Graco brought them down a lot, while I went up to Newburg sometimes.

> **FLASHBACK:** There was a agency called Louis Agency that offered summer jobs in Upstate New York for people down on their luck. It was on 42nd Street and 9th Avenue, in back of the Port Authority. From there you can be sent up into the mountains, buy your cigarettes and things and have your own room at the same time up there. I like having my own room. They sent me to Pine View Hotel for the summer in Monticello, New York. I stayed there for three weeks. It was okay. The following summer I went to

another hotel. I cleaned the grounds and hotel lobby. It was nice for the first three or five years, but then there developed problems with ex-cons working for the company. They were stealing, raping girls and running from the police. Eventually the company closed because of this.

FLASHBACK: When I was Upstate working in the summer jobs I met a young lady. I won't name her, but we had a very short affair. She would buy me clothes and things. When I got back to the city I found out that Lenny had the same girlfriend.

FLASHBACK: In the early 70s my father broke his leg in two places and his jaw. Ma and I rode out there. She had a 22 gun, although she didn't use it. It didn't have a firing pin. We told my father to, "leave everyone alone Loni!" He was in Brooklyn Hospital for a month.

FLASHBACK: A girlfriend of Auntie Fray .flew in from New York to see Auntie. I told her she went Upstate to see her son Wendell who was in jail there. I went about six or eight times Upstate to see Wendell. After all, I changed his diapers.

FLASHBACK: I cry for my mother. I cry for all mothers that had that happen to them. I cry for all my mothers who have had a man hit them. A man is not a man when they put hands on a woman the year was 1984 ma decided to move to Milwaukee wi she said she got tired of new york. She has been coming to the midwest sense the early 70 s after about a few weeks she called me to say she found a job down town she really was happy and I was happy for her so after about to months she called me to say she found apt first floor, so she was spending time with her daughter and hew father. Ma was in ny when my friend jay died it was in 1986.

FLASHBACK: In 1986 I began to have severe problems with my health. While this was going on I began to have problems with breathing. I didn't have any health insurance, but I was a veteran with an honorable discharge and so I was able to take advantage of the VA system. They found that I had chronic bronchitics.

In 1987 I took a course in recording in downtown Manhattan that cost me $200. That was a lot of money for me! Just as I was ready to make my record I got really sick right after I had the flu. I couldn't get enough breathe to sing. So I paid for that record. Well, move on Lucky.

FLASHBACK: Now my kids Van and Cherry were now 14 and 12, it was 1988. Their mother told me that they were giving her the fever. She had to put her foot down, makes some rules in the house. She told me that it was now my turn to take care of them. But she sent them one at a time to her grandmother's, which was only a few blocks from where she lived in Newburg. I saw them off and on during this time.

FLASHBACK: So now I was homeless in 1987, staying with my father in Brooklyn, but after three days we didn't get along. I came back to Manhattan and got a job as a cleaner for downtown office buildings. I rented a room from a friend who had an extra room. He lived on 125th Street by Broadway. He was the super for that building. Tommy was on methadone, was as thin as a stick, his ribs and hip bones so pronounced that it was hard to look at him for sympathy pain. I gave him a record player, but someone stole it. All in all he was a nice guy. He shared his food money and gave me pocket money now and then. I wanted to get him out here to Milwaukee years later, but he wouldn't come.

The crack heads in the building were out of control. There was a guy standing there with a hatchet and a ski mask, and they knew me. People would come from out of the area to buy crack in the building and the place was rat infested, with rats crawling up the outside of the building to get in. The FBI came and caught a buyer trying to get $40 worth of crack and killed him, putting a chain around his neck and dropped him off the side of the roof. Some other guys in the building were doing crack with this other guy and found out that he was gay. They tossed him out the back third floor window in Harlem for being gay. No one found him for three days. He walked with two canes and dark glasses after that.

The place was full of crack heads so I would just work second shift. After about a month I had to leave there. It was just too much for me at this time. The final straw was when these guys wanted me to take part in "a train" on a young woman, that's gang rape. I went to Auntie Fray's house on 110th Street of Lenox Avenue. Auntie and Uncle said I could stay there. After that I got a room. All in all I was bascally homeless for three years, from 1987-1990. I had an accident case pending and it came through in 1990, which gave me enough to find housing. But during those three years my health was real bad, getting worse in fits and starts until the symptoms wouldn't go away anymore.

> **FLASHBACK:** My father had a habit of putting me out of his apartment from 1975-1980s. It was in the summer of 1975 that me and my girlfriend Dawn and her little boy Joey were sleeping in his living room. He came home and put on all the lights telling me to "Get out of my house!" I said okay. He had been drinking again. It was 3 A.M. It meant a long way back to Harlem, but no sweat.

He had done this to me before a few years ago. My daughter was going to LIW College in downtown Brooklyn. The school was having a coming out party where they sing and party. It was a family affair: I, my father, my Auntie Fraye and Cherry's other granddad were there. It was a nice show. She sang the song "I'll be Dreaming". When it was all over, we met in the lobby. Grace gave her some money to hang with her friends, so my father thought she was coming with us. He said that he had cooked a big meal and made a cake. Cherry went with her friends. The rest of us went to my father's house. We had bought something to drink and wine. So we all had a few drinks and we ate. Then Cherry's other granddad said he had to go, so I walked him back to the train station. He caught the D train, as it was closer to his place. When I got back Grace and Auntie had gone to bed, and my father was out. So I pulled out my folding bed (he had a small apartment) and went to bed. We were all sleeping real good when father came back in saying, "Get the hell out of my place. Auntie and I got right up. I had a knife under my pillow. He pulled out a knife on me. Auntie and Grace were crying. They pushed me out into the hallway without my clothes. Then they pushed my clothes out into the hallway where I promptly put them on. Auntie and Grace got dressed and the three of us had to walk a long way to the train station. Thank God we left.

> **FLASHBACK:** My father was going with this woman in the area She could not cook. Then he had other girlfriends, their ages didn't matter. One morning while I was sleeping at my father's place I discovered he was sleeping with a young girl when, around daybreak, she tried to pass over me to get to the door. My father was trying to burn the woman! He was talking loud, saying, "Lucky she got my money out of my pants!" As she left she said to me, "Your father is crazy!" I answered, "Yes. I know."

My father has black outs where he'll do something and won't remember it. That's why, when I slept over at Lonis house, I would sleep with one eye open.

? My father's two brothers, his older brother Big Lucky tried to talk to my girlfriend this one time when Grace and I was living in a brownstone place on South Portland Street. So people would tell me to let go of the thought of y mother and Auntie. I don't want anyone telling me anything, because I have stepped up to the plate again and again and again. I know that there is a place in heaven for me. It is not always like father like son. I broke the cycle on that, God bless! I never lost sight of my being human.

FLASHBACK: While I was a cook in Upstate New York for the YMCA, a bat flew into the Mess Hall. All of the kids were scared so everyone left the building. Another cook went and got a shake and that it. Bats are blind in the daylight. So all the kids came back and we shared lunch.

FLASHBACK: I had a room on 121st Street from 1983-1985 for $35 a week. It was a brownstone building with my apartment on the second floor in front. I was working as a security guard at Manhattan Valley. It was a row of 15 houses being built. I worked from 3:30 PM to 8 AM, making $450 a week. It was okay for awhile. After six months I left that job. I got word that the Apollo Theater was getting ready to open. I went there with two other guys. We were all hired as ushers, but needed a black jacket and white shirt. My landlord lent me his jacket. I had my tie and white shirt. I was in charge of taking people to their seats with a little flashlight. It was cool. By working there I've seen so many stars. I was there for the Motown Reunion Show. It was heavy. These cats had it made.

The only thing about this job was that after some time new people came in and took over the Apollo. We had to work longer hours anywhere from six to twelve hours on our feet. Because of this I left the Apollo after six months. I didn't like all of the new rules: I had to tell people to put out their cigarettes and pipes; go downstairs to the men's room, and; tell them to put away their coke cans. When I left my two friends stayed. One left a month later, but the other stayed and eventually was in charge of everything, working there four or five years.

My picture was in the window of the Apollo for two years. I went some time later to them and asked to buy that picture. They told me that there had been a fire and that the picture had been burned.

> **FLASHBACK:** In 1988 and '89 I performed at a supper club named Gian-Luca. It was on 74th Street on the Uptown side of the street. It was right next to the Beacon theater. This was on Broadway. For once someone paid to see me and around ten more people. It was a shower singers show for $8 at the door and $10 at the table. Each of us sang a song. I have video tapes of myself. I had fun. For my first show I sang "Teach Me Tonight" and music like Billy Joel's "New York State of Mind," and a song called "At This moment by Billy Vera and the Beaters. My very best song of all was "My funny Valentine" in the music style of Mr. Frank Sinatra. He is a jazz singer. First I am a jazz singer, then pop singer and finally R & B. I think back that I wasn't consistent in my career: as a singer or an actor or a person. I was always finding women on my watch, single or married.

Lenny's grandfather and grandmother lived in Upstate, New York in Beacon, N.Y. Across the river from Newburg, 60 miles up the Hudson River. My mother met up with some guy named Sonny. He had high cheek bones and very dark skin. He was around 55 or so and wore his hair slicked back in the style of the day. Meanwhile my Auntie Fraye met a real nice light skinned guy who was almost white. My Auntie and her new friend named Freddy also got a room there. I used to run away again. I was around seven years old. I had run away from my grandmother's in Fort Greene Projects in downtown Brooklyn. There used to be an L train on Myrtle Avenue. I would go to Jay Street. I think my father got tired of coming to get me on the train.

FLASHBACK: When I was working at the Apollo Carmen came up from Florida. I got her two free tickets to see a show. This was in '84 or '85. I also got my mother two free tickets to see a show.

FLASHBACK: When I was at the Apollo for the Motown Review I got to see the Four Tops, the Temps, Mary Wells, Diana Ross, Sara Von, Jesse Jackson and his people, the Barge Family, Jennifer Holiday, (the mayor of New York David Dinkins showed up), and Sammy Davis Jr.,...just anybody who was any one in music was there. They had the street closed off even around the corner on 126th Street. That was good. I will never forget who I saw.

FLASHBACK: Now you only live once and you have to be good to yourself. So after I left the Apollo I did jobs here and there, on and off the books. By now it was '86 and while I was living on 121st Street for 18 months I had a few people stay with me, because of one thing or another.

My father was to stay with me for a month, because he cut my uncle. Aunt Lil from the Bronx didn't like that and they called me to go uptown to see what was going on in the Bronx with Uncle and dad. When I arrived up there the lights were out and I called, "Uncle, where are you?" He was sitting on the floor. I saw my father Loni with a wine bottle in one hand and a knife in the other. I had to act fast. I asked Loni, "What the hell did you do to Uncle?!" I could see that Uncle was not bleeding too bad. I could see the cut, it was not that bad.

FLASHBACK: I had to talk Loni out of the apartment and into the hall. As soon as he got in the hall I took the wine and threw it out and then got that knife from him. Loni gets black outs when he drinks, so I had him come to stay with me for two or three weeks. I had a loveseat and my bed folded up once I got up.

A friend of mine needed some place to sleep. His name is Dennis. He is a school teacher and an actor. I said as long as my landlord didn't mind it was alright. He got up early and didn't return until 9 PM. After two months Dennis paid me $150. Then he thanked me.

Another friend named Jay asked to stay with me again. I asked the landlord and got permission. Jay was very sick. He had to move from where he was living. So Jay had to stay with me for about a month and a half. He paid me.

Soon after Jay got too sick to stay with me anymore, some other friends came and got Jay, taking him to a hospital Uptown on Broadway. I went to see him, but he couldn't see me. I knew he could hear me. I told him to hang in there and I left. About three days later jay died. It was '86, because ma was here visiting Auntie Fraye.

> FLASHBACK: I took Jay's death really hard. I started crying so loud. Ma was there. I got so damn mad that I put my right hand through the landlord's glass front door. I didn't care. I went upstairs and got my TV, brought it down and threw it across the street. A family member of the landlord's came from the back apartment in the building carrying a knife. Ma told him, "If you cut my son you will have to cut me!"

My hand was bleeding all over the place. I went and got it stitched up. Then ma said, "Son, come back with me for awhile." So I had to leave and went to say hello to Auntie and told her that I would see her soon.

> FLASHBACK: By now it was '87. I went to Milwaukee with ma. She had a big apartment on the first floor. I took a cab to see my cousin G-G and her daughters Flash and Mary, and G-Gs son Rock. I stayed for about a month and had a picture I.D. Made in Milwaukee. Then I had to get back to New York City.

FLASHBACK: I had had a case pending. Now I found out that I had won the case. I would have to wait 3-4 weeks to see any money from it. I went to Brooklyn to stay with dad, but as always we didn't get along when he started drinking. So I went to Auntie Frays house.

FLASHBACK: In the years between '88-'89, staying between Brooklyn and Auntie Frays house, Uncle Freddy had been getting real sick. He had been in three hospitals already. When he was back home he could smell cigarette smoke down the hall and it just made him sick all over again. In late '89 he went back into the hospital. They had a cat. I put the cat in a box with water and food, and took the box to the park.

FLASHBACK: I cleaned the closet and painted the place, and I got Auntie a phone so that she could keep in touch with Wendell in Upstate jail, and so that ma could call her from time to time. It was 1990 when I got my settlement. It was over $12,000.

FLASHBACK: I had a P.O.Box. My check was in it and it was 10 AM. I got so scared I called Auntie up and asked her to come by cab to 125th Street. I took my check to the check cashing places where I had to show all kinds of I.D. Before they cashed it...all in $20 bills. That was a lot of bills, two paper bags full!

FLASHBACK: Auntie came up. She said a good friend of hers and Uncle would hold it for me. So I went back downtown, asked him and he said it would be okay. I gave him a $50 bill to buy his grandson a savings bond. Now I was in auntie's place, brought her something to cook in the next two days. Later I got my money back. I called Rita and Sam. They are very good friends with ma and I said Sam couldn't see that good. So I went to pick him up. Sam took me to his bank, the Apple Bank on East 125th Street and Lexington Avenue near the train station. They knew Sam, so he talked to them about putting my money in their bank. I opened a savings account. I gave Sam a few dollars for helping me out.

FLASHBACK: Later that day Auntie and I went to visit Uncle. He was so so now. I called a friend of mine who I rented a room from and told him to come over and hang out with us. After leaving Harlem Hospital on 135th Street and Lenox Avenue we brought something to drink. I brought some pills to sleep. So we had a good time.

FLASHBACK: Auntie and I got to her house and I wasn't feeling any pain. In the building the bathroom was in the hallway, so neither of us locked the apartment door behind us. We were sleeping. Auntie Fraye said that she saw the front door being closed for some reason and saw someone carrying my boom box for some reason. It was black and had six speakers. Auntie got it back. I jumped up, went to check my pants pockets. I had $400 in there. They didn't get to that money

FLASHBACK: Later the next day I told ma what had happened to us over the phone. Boy was she upset about that. Ma said we could have been killed in there. So we went to see Uncle. He was in Roosevelt Hospital. To get there we had to get on the Tram Way. It went up ten stories high, right next to the bridge.

FLASHBACK: It was early April 1990 now when we got to see Uncle. He said, "Lucky, for God's sake get your Aunt out of here. Get her out there with her sister, your ma." I said I will and we left. We could see that Uncle wasn't breathing too well. Two days later the phone rang. They said that Uncle Freddy had died. I was at Rita and Sam's house about 10 blocks away. I got down there to see Auntie, whether she was alright or not. It was April.

FLASHBACK: I called ma in Milwaukee. She said that she would be here in a few days. She was working. Uncle Freddy was Wendell's fathers. Now, Wendell was upstate doing time. Ma and I did all the running around, making the funeral arrangements.

FLASHBACK: The funeral was to be the following week, the third week of April. When they brought his son down from jail he was in chains-hands and legs. The funeral was at 135th Street in Harlem, N.Y. After a week ma flew back to Milwaukee. I was just staying close to Auntie now. In the next two weeks I bought Auntie a one way ticket to Milwaukee and gave her $50 along with some cigarettes. I said, "Auntie, you have 4 days to say goodbye to your friends here." She said, "Okay."

FLASHBACK: I had a room down on 34th Street YMCA. It was costing me too much money so I found an apartment on 137th Street and Convent Avenue. It was a small place. It had a bed with a dresser, a table and two chairs, and had one window. It was okay. It was in a brownstone third floor back apartment.

FLASHBACK: When I first got the place I had to pay her $1,100 in cash. Only then did I get the key. I had been in Milwaukee for three or four months by then and gramps gave me his boom box. It was big. Lenny and I took my boom box and I had Miss Rita's 5" TV. Not paying attention two young guys in the front apartment saw me bringing the boom box and the little TV in. When I came back the next day to move in the door was open, my boom box and little TV was gone. It was those two guys who saw us leave, which happened to be the landlady's grandson. He was on crack. She gave me her 19" color TV. I said good, okay.

FLASHBACK: The day before Auntie was to leave for Milwaukee she and Lenny came up to my place. I made something to eat and bought some beer for us. The next morning when we all woke up Auntie was already packed. I called a cab. I had a phone put in my apartment.

FLASHBACK: Before Auntie left and Uncle was still getting around, I had a cleaning job. I was like a boy cleaner for a lady who lived on Spring Street, not too far from the World Trade Center. I would go there once every Wednesday for 2 ½ hours and made $40. After a month she fired me and next she hired me back at a $10 raise, so now I made $50.

When I came back Uptown I always stopped to see Auntie and Uncle, sometimes giving Uncle $10 or $15 so that he could play his numbers. I'd check on auntie, she'd be watching TV or talking to some of her girlfriends in the building. I would go back to the store and get some beer for the two of us.

FLASHBACK: You know it always gave me a good feeling when I did stop to see them. I didn't have my own place. This would be 1986-'87.

FLASHBACK: It's now 1990 and Auntie has gotten to Milwaukee. Okay, I know that ma was happy to see her sister. Ma told me, gramps always told them to stay together always.

Now I was drinking a lot daily, smoking weed, and trying to do something with my singing. I had a keyboard. A friend of mine with whom I was staying gave it to me "before someone stole it." So I was talking to someone who said he knew how to play the keyboard, but I had to buy him some beer. He played the song "She's Out Of My Life," which I knew well, and he could play it without reading music.

> FLASHBACK: It was cool, but now I found myself drinking with him and drinking and just being a damn fool. So I told him not to come around any more.

> FLASHBACK: It was in early August 1990 that I was mugged. The woman I was working for as a Boy Friday, I told her I was moving to Milwaukee in September sometime. Julie was her name. She said that she was moving to L.A. anyway. That worked for both of us. She gave me a small birthday party with her two coworkers. I said goodbye. I was starting to mail my things to ma ahead of me, but I was running out of money.

So now my birthday came and went. I was still drinking. I had a one way ticket to Milwaukee. I was to leave on October 4th, 1990. I didn't have any jackets, nothing heavy to wear. I had nothing, just my Social Security card. Lenny came over and spent the night. We always talked about our family, so we had a few beers and then it was October 4th.

> FLASHBACK: It is time for Lucky to leave New York City, so Lenny road with me down to Pennsylvania Station. I said goodbye to Lenny, or see you later, rather than goodbye.

> FLASHBACK: The train ride was okay. It was cold at nighttime, but I fell asleep. When I woke up it was daylight. We would soon be in Milwaukee, home of cheese and beer.

> FLASHBACK: I got to Milwaukee around 3 PM Central Time. I'll have to remember that. When I got off there was ma and Auntie, Rock, Ge-Ge's son. When we arrived at ma's place I learned that Auntie had gotten an apartment across

the hall from her. There I was with my family whom I loved so much. They sent to the store to get some beer. It was only a few blocks away, but I still got lost. A friend of ma's came to get me in his car. It was just that one time that I got lost. It's a good feeling to be around family. My cousin Rock gave me a jacket. It was cool outside. One by one I got to see the rest of my family. I saw my sister a few days later. She was working and going to school.

I went walking a few blocks and got to Wisconsin Avenue. I found a Veterans Center there on 34th Street and Wisconsin Avenue. There I was seen by Ms. Wendy M.S. and Ph.D. I started seeing her 2-3 times a week from October 1990 to September 1991. Once I started seeing Ms. windy I did keep most of my appointments right from the first week I was in Milwaukee. I didn't know I was holding all these feelings inside of me, much of it about my father: how I had to go check on him all of the time when I was in New York. So by now I had a V.A. Appeal going on. One thing that I did find out was that I had a personality disorder. Somewhere along the way I developed this. I don't know when. I know that while I was in the army I started to get headaches on and off, getting dizzy a lot, and my nerves were shaky also. So, to put it in a nut shell I suffer from Schizophrenia Disorder-Residual Type Chronic, Personality Disorder, and let's not leave out back pains and headaches.

I had been going to see her now for about a year. A lot of things were about my father, always coming to his aide, even after I came to Milwaukee. I told Ms. windy how my father almost died from being stabbed in the face, and all those bite marks on his legs, all that damn blood I had to clean up. I told her so many times, I told him, "I'm not a fighter!"

FLASHBACK: I told him over and over that I like to write poetry. I like to write songs and work with wood. I guess I wasn't like him. No, that's not me. Why the hell did my father feel he had to live his life through me?! It was damn hard living for him and living for me, not counting taking care of my Auntie and my mother, my two mothers whom I love very much. I will leave that to you. What do you think? No, I like to put my feelings into my poetry or put them into a song or dance. I can do that. I have done that.

FLASHBACK: Meanwhile I entered a radio contest, a black radio station. It was early in 1991. I won a shopping spree. I know That I felt like a little kid with that shopping spree. And at the same time the same radio station had their first black Awards Show. So I chose to dance and I did at the Milwaukee Area Technical College in Milwaukee. Most of my family came. I was 42 years old. I didn't win any money. I think a little boy won the contest for doing M.J. dance. The 1st prize was $500.

FLASHBACK: About six of us came back to my apartment.

FLASHBACK: In 1991 I started building a platform that was 82" x 82". I had just gotten my apartment. I had won my appeal from the Social Security Administration. My father was here after he got stabbed. It was summertime when I was lucky to get a one bedroom apartment in the same building as ma and Auntie. It was a 4-plex apartment building. I was still going back to New York to see my Aunt Lil in the Bronx. I was there in 1992 having dinner at Aunt Lil's house when I got a call on a 3-way that my friend died. The one that worked with me at the Apollo. He even won twice on the Showtime At The Apollo. That really had me good. I needed a drink. I was in New York at the right time. His mother had a service for him a few days later. It was on Prospect Avenue in the Bronx, N.Y. I just remember when we worked together.

FLASHBACK: We used to play cards a lot.

FLASHBACK: In 1992 I heard that the show Star Search was coming to Milwaukee. Wouldn't you know it, star Search called me to audition on my birthday September 12th up at a place called North Ridge Mall. I didn't know how to get there so I took a cab there.

FLASHBACK: When I heard that Star Search had called me I was so happy that I baked two cakes, one for me and one for a little girl next door. Her birthday was the same day.

So now it was my turn to go up there. There were about 400-500 people there. That didn't bother me at all. I sang a few bars of Ray Charles' "Georgia Is On My Mind." They said, "Okay Lucky. We'll be in touch."

FLASHBACK: Well, that was a chance in a lifetime. I'm not shy when it comes to singing or dancing. By now I was 43 years old.

FLASHBACK: When I was still in Harlem I did sing at the Baby Grand Club that was on 125th Street. It was down the street from the Apollo. I did some work for the Hansberry, Sands Theater in 1999. I was with Capital Productions. I did make it in New York. After all we only go around here once and one time is enough time for all of us, rich or poor. Don't you think so?

FLASHBACK: My name is Lucky. I cry for my mother. I cry for all mothers. I cry for all women who some man or men have put their hands on. My name is Lucky. What's your's? Well, how do you do?

FLASHBACK: I was diagnosed with Post Traumatic Stress Disorder (PTSD) in 1991 after going into a psychiatric ward for two weeks.

FLASHBACK: In fall of 1992 I flew to New York to see all of my cousins and my great Aunt Lil in the Bronx. Everyone there was okay. They went downtown to Broadway. I always go down there to get my sheet music. So I'm in Brooklyn to try to talk my father into moving to Milwaukee where his family was, but no dice. All Loni wanted was a drink or a woman, any woman. So I came back to Milwaukee.

FLASHBACK: Wherever my two mothers are, I am not too far away from them. I guess I never grew out of being with either of them, with my Auntie or my mother who I thought made me safe. So I was going to the doctor with Auntie Fraye. The doctor told ma and her that Auntie had pancreatitus and that had to open her up. So the next month Auntie went to the hospital. It was 1993, in the winter. In November Auntie got a Christmas tree from some friend around the corner that was nice.

FLASHBACK: My mother and Auntie Fray had their own friends before I was born. Auntie's friend was Norma from Harlem. They knew each other about 50 years now. Anyway, when Norma heard about Auntie's health she flew to Milwaukee from New York to see her friend. Now that is what I call a friend. It doesn't get any better than that. When Norma walked into Auntie's bedroom you should have seen the look on Auntie's face! I wouldn't trade that for anything. Auntie was happy. She had to stay in bed for awhile.

FLASHBACK: Now ma's best friend is Diane. Norma and Diane are sister-in-laws.

FLASHBACK: In 1993 my white female friend came to visit me. We talked and talked. We bought a case of beer. I told her that people don't sit outside like they do in New York and drink. So we went inside to Auntie's house. She had carpet and we sat on the carpet together.

Oh, yes, Pat and I got drunk right there on the floor. Pat has two sons that were grown and two girls that were 16 and 10 years old. So I just said, "You want to get married Pat?" She said, "Okay." You see, we've been friends since 1968 when I first went into the army. So I thought I would be helping them get out of the South Bronx. We made a date to get married in December 1994. I asked around looking for a bigger place. My luck was running well. The house where we lived had a half a house, a duplex, right in back of where I, ma and Auntie lived. I talked to my play sisters <u>Dee Foxi</u> and <u>Lilian</u>. They know my whole family and we know theirs also.

> **FLASHBACK:** Ma and I were watching out for Auntie who by this time was not feeling very well. I went upstairs to my apartment, because Lenny was on the scene now. Lenny didn't change at all from New York City. And his ways,...I'll leave that one alone.

> **FLASHBACK:** In 1992 I had won my V.A. appeal, when I won my V.A. appeal I got back pay of $12,000. I asked ma which one I should keep or give up? I gave back the S.S.I. check and kept the V.A. one. That was more money anyway. I didn't want to cheat the state of Wisconsin, right, and I got $7,000 from this other company later that year. So Pat and her kids came on the Greyhound bus, but wait...

> **FLASHBACK:** When I said that Auntie wasn't feeling well, ma, Lenny and I took Auntie to the doctor. It seemed she had a growth down the back of her throat. The doctor told her to visit her family. If she wanted to live six months to a year she would have to have her esophagi operated on. Otherwise she had only three months.

FLASHBACK: Auntie had the operation. We were all at the hospital. I spent the night and had brought my small TV. I went back and forth to see how Auntie was doing. Her son Lenny was over there looking after her. Ma came up a few times to have coffee with Pat.

It was time to get the girls back in school. Kelly is 16 and Tina is 10 years old. Kelly was in the 10th grade and Tina in the 4th grade, the school was not far from the house.

I was still going to the Veterans Center on Wisconsin Avenue.

It's easy to talk to Ms. windy. I see now that I am in a depression mode. I like some isolation. Sometimes I would cancel my appointment, but I always made up for not coming before moving on.

FLASHBACK: Back to my wife and step kids. Well we both found out that Kelly skipped classes smoking cigarettes. I went over to the School of Arts. Her teacher said that Kelly thought she was all that and then some. So I talked to her mother about that. She didn't want to hear that, so I let it go. As two weeks passed Kelly was still doing the same thing...in and out of school. I thought my wife and I would be close, but as life would have it, it didn't happen.

FLASHBACK: Mind was on my Auntie right then. I knew my mother was worried about her, but her health was going down hill.

FLASHBACK: Right after New Years 1995 Auntie had to go back into the hospital. This time the doctor took out the feeding tube. My wife and I were not seeing eye to eye, so between me looking out for ma and trying to be the stand up man in my household it didn't work. It was February 1995 on the 10th when Kelly got kicked out of school for two days for walking out. My friends asked me what was wrong? I said, "Nothing, it's nothing wrong."

FLASHBACK: No sooner had they brought Auntie out of the hospital when they said they had to have her back in to remove her stomach in order to save her life for now. Ma screamed so loud, I got messed up in my head. My mother's younger sister came in from out of town. The doctors performed the operation and they put a tube into her.

FLASHBACK: It was Auntie's esophagus that had to be taken out and 10 minutes later they told ma that to remove her stomach it would be necessary to put a small tube into her small intestines. I was thinking to myself, this was no time to lose it Lucky. Be strong for your family.

FLASHBACK: Auntie had to have the operations to allow her to live another 6-8 months.

FLASHBACK: When I got that big place around the corner Lenny brought Auntie around there. Lenny had to pick her up. I was on the 2nd floor. She saw my place and said, "Lucky, all this is your's." I said, "Yes, it is Auntie." That meant a lot to me to see Auntie see my new place.

Now there was nothing in it yet, but it had 3 bedrooms, 2 living rooms, a dining room, and a big kitchen. I had to buy a big stove and ice box. So I put in cable, brought two more beds, and I had my mother's wooden table to eat on. My mother's friend gave me another table. It was glass on the inside and black wood on the outside. It was nice. That same friend gave me a lamp with a black shade.

FLASHBACK: When I did my apartment in the same building as ma and Auntie, my play sister Dee drove me to look at something for my living room. The store was called American Store. It was pretty big by Wisconsin terms. I saw a round black bar with two stools. It was nice so why not stay with the color black. I picked out a couch with the same color that I found there. I even found a black leather chair that had an ottoman.

So ma didn't want to see Auntie like that. She couldn't talk or move, but I knew she could hear me when I went to see her. I gave her a kiss on the forehead and said, "I love you Aunt Fraye. We will always love you." The last time that I and Ge-Ge's daughter went to see her was February 21st. Something told me she wouldn't make it too much longer now. The hospital called ma early on the 22nd at 3 AM to say Aunt Fray had passed away.

FLASHBACK: You see my Uncle Freddy's birthday was February 22nd. I know that he came and got her. That's Wendell's father. Ma and Lenny made the funeral arrangements. It was a very sad day for our family, especially for ma. Her father told them to always stay together. Always. I was by ma's side the whole time.

Not long after that, it was around the end of February, I was drinking and told my wife Pat and her two daughters to get out of the house. Well they got out in a hurry too, right over to my mother's house around the corner. I called over there to tell them to come back home. I knew the girls had to go to school. Not long after that I told Pat that I was moving out. She said, go ahead and took her wedding ring off and threw it on the floor. I picked it up and the next day sold it. I stayed with ma for the time being. A dew days later I went back and got my 25" TV, my fish tank, and my wood and clothes. After a month with my mother I was able to get my old apartment back upstairs.

FLASHBACK: Pat's older daughter disrespected me anyway and her mother didn't say anything about it. Our marriage was over before it got started. I did help them to get out of the Bronx anyway. I guess I'm set in my own ways now. So now I was keeping my eye on ma and making sure she was alright. g-G would come over sometimes.

One morning my sister Lucy came by to take us out to get something to eat. So I was getting ready to fly to New York City to see my father when I got word that he was sick. I could kill two birds with one stone.

First I went to Brooklyn to see dad. Yes, I went to see my father. He didn't look good at all. I told him that I was riding up to the Bronx o see my great aunt Lil, my cousins and Wendell too. After I told Wendell about Loni being sick he rode out to Brooklyn with me. Loni had a home tender. She told me that Loni would last 6 months or so. I just put my head down for a moment. She said, I should tell him to move out to Milwaukee where his family was. He said, okay, after he kept his doctors' appointments. He started mailing his things to Milwaukee like I had done. This was right before the 4th of July.

I went downtown to look at some music sheets. It was on 49th Street and Broadway. I bought some N.Y. Tee shirts for some friend of mine.

I kept thinking about my father. He was real dark and his little bit of hair was coming out. I spoke to my father's other sister whom my grandmother raised as her own. I told her what Loni was going to do. She was happy. You see, she was still young with two daughters of her own. I told Loni it was costing me a lot of money flying back and forth.

I had just enough time to take a bus to see my kids' mother and my daughter Cherry who had a baby girl herself. The baby was four or five years old. I spent the night. I know Grace was glad to see me. You see, when the kids were 12 and 10 she said, now it's my turn to take care of them. I took some pictures of the baby, came back to Brooklyn to meet up with Wendell as he would help dad start packing to mail them to me in a few weeks.

Well, it was now August 1996. I told ma that Loni was moving here for good. She was glad. g-G was glad too. I couldn't get it out of my head what my father's nurse had said to me: 6 month or less to live. My father had more lives than a cat. Dig it? Dad had a washing machine. He told Wendell to come and get it. Dad gave him his keys to his apartment there in Brooklyn. Loni got to Milwaukee on August 15th, 1996.

I and G-Gs son Rock went to pick Loni up at the airport. He took Midwest Airlines. They had to get a wheelchair for him. It seems he had gotten darker, all of his little bit of hair came out. Never the less, he's my father. I found a TV in the backyard. I brought it in and it worked, only the bottom 2" were black. Otherwise it was something for him to watch in the bedroom. I brought a new dresser for his things. My mother was glad to see him. She had cooked a big meal. Dad had my bedroom. It was nice and quiet there. I told him to get a good nights sleep.

The next morning I took him first to the bank and had him put me down as his Power of Attorney. Then we went to the courthouse to get his I.D. Made and then off to the hospital to set up all of his appointments and a heart doctor. That took two hours. By 5 PM coming in we were both tired.

He got it all done in one week. Do you know that in two weeks Loni was looking better. He could walk with his cane to the store and back.

> FLASHBACK: I could see that Loni was getting better. He was talking a mile a minute. Anyway, I was not on talking terms with sis and her daughter. He didn't know what was going down. Ma said that she could get him his own apartment right next door in the other building near us.

My birthday came up and dad made me a cake, cooked some greens and fried chicken, and bought some beer. I could see in dad's eyes that he was happy, I mean really happy here with me, his wife with whom he had remained friends after all these years and his daughter Luci. Right after my birthday he said, "Son, I want to get to the bottom of this, what's going down between you and your sister."

Loni got the apartment right next door in the other building. He had his tape player. He bought a small TV. A friend of ma's had a table and four chairs for the living room. Loni bought a bed set. We started playing cards.

Dad asked me to make a food list so he could cook a big meal for ma, myself, and my sister, so that he could try to get things started with us.

It was a week later, the third week in September, when dad called him, "Lucky! Come here! I can't stand up. I'm sick to my stomach. I can't hold anything down." He was in that apartment for less than two month. Now he was really sick. I called all of the family. I called ma to tell her what was going down with my father. She said, "Stick with your father, Lucky." I said, "You know I will ma." So they came. Off we went to the hospital. Sometimes you have to tell the doctor what is going on with your body.

They took dad upstairs to his room on the 4th floor. What I didn't want to hear was my father's cancer had come back. They told the family about Loni. The next day ma and I went down there. Again the doctor couldn't see what was wrong, why he now couldn't talk. My mother told the doctor, "Loni has had a stroke." She told the doctor to take some blood tests. Loni was in there until about the middle of October 1996.

> FLASHBACK: The doctor told ma that Loni would have to go into a nursing home. He went where gramps was to stay for six months.

> FLASHBACK: I went there often to see both of them. Sometimes I think that the people that I love...something always happens to them. So far, not Loni. The days went by and then a couple of weeks. Now it was cold outside. I went to see Loni and gramps. I stayed for about 2 ½ hours. I got home and the phone rang. It was the nursing home telling me I should get back out there, because Loni's breathing was slowing down. So I called my sister and she came to pick us up. We got there at about 6 PM. We were there

for about 15 minutes when my father stopped breathing altogether.

We all started to cry, me, ma and my sister. We cried out loud. I didn't know my mother still loved him. We gathered his things and left.

FLASHBACK: My mother and sister made the funeral arrangements which was fine with me. It was December 23rd, 1996. On that day it was raining and I wasn't feeling well. At the funeral home Lenny got up to say something about Loni. I was too sick to get up there. Lenny said, "Don't nobody forget about uncle Loni."

Now we had to get rid of his things in his apartment. Ma sold the highriser and the chair to someone in the building. Ma also sold his bedroom set. I took the tape player over to my place. I had to sell the table set and TV. I think it was taking its told on ma and me. I <u>look to God to keep me going</u>. I do not want to forget about God or close his phone down.

FLASHBACK: Back when Auntie Fray died I sang a song for her and I was ready to cry again, so we said The Lord's Prayer.

FLASHBACK: My father was 65 when he died. I'm glad I did what I did...there was no time to think, just do it. Take care of your mother and father. So now it is me and ma.

FLASHBACK: Love is always the Light, the light of the day. I went to New York City to see my great aunt Lil and my cousins up in the Bronx, stopped down in Harlem on Central Park West where ma used to live. It was good to see old friends again, to walk around Auntie's old building on 110th Street.

So now it's 1997. Ma is thinking about moving, but only because someone broke into her apartment through the window.

She lived on the ground floor. G-G would come by from time to time. G-Gs- daughter Flash would come by also bringing her some ice cream and a soda.

> **FLASHBACK:** Sometimes I think to myself, Is this my world that I'm living in or is this really your world that I am passing through like a thief in the night?

> **FLASHBACK:** If I may, back in 1966 my kid's mother and I, and an older male friend of the family named Kent all went down to the Apollo to see a show called The Jewel Box Review. It was like 24 men dressed up as women. They would sing and dance and were damn good. They all looked and acted just like women. And one woman dressed like a man that was the host of the show. We all enjoyed the show.

> **FLASHBACK:** Back in the mid '80s Loni had a drinking friend. He was knocking on the door. Loni didn't hear him and shouted through the door that he was sleeping. So the guy said he was Larry, and went and got some gasoline. He threw it under Loni's door and set fire to it, but it backfired on Larry. He was a dark skinned guy, real small, so he got burned on his neck and one side of his face. Wouldn't you know it, they became close friends until Larry died.

> **FLASHBACK:** So ma found a place across town. It was for people 62 and older. It was around the end of May and she had to move June 1st, 1997.

We were watching TV when the news came on and announced that a stepmother was being charged in the death of her six year old stepdaughter. A few hours later a call came in and someone told ma that it was our family member who was killed. Her name was Kim. My mother screamed and dropped the phone, starting to cry. That's when I found out about it. The stepmother's name was Lynn. We found out she didn't like the little girl, because she looked so much like her mother who died two weeks after she was born. Ma didn't want to go to court with us. So after a few days, while in court, the judge gave her 15 years for taking a little girl's life. So the girl's father and e-G, who was her grandmother, made the arraignment. Ma didn't want to go. I could understand. The funeral was very large. It was another dark day for our family.

I talked ma into not moving until June 1st, 1997, because I found a new apartment that was also downtown. But in the meantime ma and I would keep each other company. So June 1st came and ma had G-G's son Rock and her daughter Flash to help in the moving. They had a truck. I helped out too. So ma moved out of the building where we lived all had been living together.

Her new apartment was nice. It had a big living room and was carpeted. She could do her wash right down the hallway.

> **FLASHBACK:** Myself, I just couldn't wait to move and get the hell out of there. It started out happy. I was happy that ma and Auntie were in the same building for awhile. And I got my father out of Brooklyn to come to Milwaukee to be around family. It seems my happy time was almost gone. I thought I still have my mother, her cousins, and sister here in Milwaukee.

> **FLASHBACK:** Now July 1st came and it was time for me to move out of this area before I killed somebody. I was always saying that.

> **FLASHBACK:** In 1993 or '94 I bought a gun one night around midnight. This was before Auntie died. I went outside into the street and dared anybody up and down the whole block to take me on! I don't know why I did this. Maybe because of my father and all of the pain around him that came out in my therapy sessions with Ms. wendy. Ma heard me. She was scared that I was going to kill someone

or myself. Anyway, I got rid of it. I know that I can get into my music to keep cool and calm. Sometimes I think, stop the world, I want to get off, but you know time waits for no one.

FLASHBACK: So now I moved into my new apartment downtown in a big apartment building. I was on the 6th floor of an eight story building. The apartment was okay. To my Readers that's my illustration of how I handle things when they go wrong or really go haywire. Sometimes when I wake up I look in the mirror and wonder who are you Lucky? Are you Black, Latin or good or bad. The mystery of my life. The foundation of the world that we all live in right now...not tomorrow, is gone.

FLASHBACK: I was going often to visit grandpa. He almost didn't know who I was. Well, on this one day I went to visit him we were doing good. That was July 28th. Ma got a call from the nursing home that we better get there, because gramps died in his sleep. July 28th was my father's birthday.

FLASHBACK: So I, ma, and my sister and her husband were there. We packed up his things.. My sister and ma made the funeral arrangements. It was to be July 31st, 1998. It was a sad day for our family once again. My sister and Gg- and ma. Really it was too hard. Some of gramps old friends came by to see him, telling us about when they would do some music gigs together here and up north in Wisconsin. Ma had a big oil painting of gramps on the piano. He played the Apollo in 1946 and '48, my mother told me and Lenny. So now, moving on...

FLASHBACK: It was a very good year for all the Black clubs that were in Harlem from the 1930s to 1970-'72.

FLASHBACK: Gramps and his two daughters, Mae and Fraye, and their three children...there was a big family picture of all my family with gramps sitting in the middle from 1987. I, myself, wasn't in Milwaukee and Lenny and Wendell also, the story goes on to say. But at the end of the story Earl's grandson Lucky who is a Jazz singer never heard him sing. He lives on in New York City.

FLASHBACK: It's 1999. I let a guy move in my apartment with me, because he got put out. So I thought it was cool, I'll have some company. Around the same time I made friends with a woman whose name is Laura. We started talking, meanwhile I told ma.

FLASHBACK: In 1997 I started going over to ma's place a lot. Sometimes I would spend the night and I would bring her some ice cream, and myself some cookies. So I was going back and forth from my apartment to ma's, or went to New York City to see great aunt Lil and my other cousins in the Bronx. I only stayed for 10 days.

I came back early from New York to learn that ma was sick. She was n the hospital. I unpacked my things and went to see ma. I asked her if there was anything she needed? She said, "No, son." I gave ma a kiss. I went to her apartment to check on her mail and brought her mail to her. They were just bills.

A few days later ma came home. She said there is nothing like your own bed. Okay, I said. She gave me a list for some food for her. There was a new Pick "N Save store down the street. So now it is February 1998.

FLASHBACK: That year in May Wendell and his son Marvin came to visit ma and us. Wendell had this great big suit-case. His son Marvin wouldn't go anywhere without his father, Big Head, I called him. G-G and her son came over to see Wendell. Then they all left to go see the mall, I think.

Ma was happy to see him and Big Headn.

FLASHBACK: So after a week and a half Wendell and his son left to go back to New York City. It was now June of 1998 as family went back and forth.

FLASHBACK: In 1998 the guy moved a few things into my apartment. He had lived across the hall and had gotten put out. In a few days I found out that he was smoking crack in my apartment when I was gone or over at ma's place. So ma didn't like what I was doing. The female I mentioned and I became friends. Whenever she saw my roommate she would roll her eyes all the time. My mother asked me why I was smoking crack with him? I said, No, but I lied. I found myself smoking with him.

Somehow my mother had found out. It was in winter now, almost Christmas. Ma was getting ready to go to New York City to visit. She said, "Lucky, I'm going to take you off my life insurance if you are still smoking crack with that guy."

So I was going to selling all of the things that guy had given me. He had said that I could have his floor TV, but the next day he wanted it back. I told him, no way! Then he tried to break my door open, so I let him take the damn TV. I gave him my 10 gallon fish tank with the fish in it. I said, "You have to go! Get your stuff and go!" Lenny had met him and said that he didn't trust him. So he is gone...moving on.

FLASHBACK: Let me get myself together and stop this shit. And I did. Ma came back from New York on June 2nd. The year was 2000. I met her at the airport and then took a cab back to her place. Once there she asked me if I still had that guy living with me. I said, "No, ma. I don't." So now I know that if I tell my mother something, I will keep my word.

I had to go to the V.A. Hospital to get my blood test and

checkup. My health was okay.

> **FLASHBACK:** The year 2000. This is a show tune, but the show hasn't been written yet. I bought my Karaoke tapes to keep my voice in shape all of the time. Some of the tapes I bought are Billy Joel music, music from the movie The Wiz, and three tapes of Luther Van dross and Marvin Gay types. I also bought music to sing to The Platters, Sam Cooke music, and all time great music by Frank Sinatra. To date I have 24 Karaoke tapes. I'm working on some CDs now.

So I rid myself of that roommate. Never! No more! I can't have no one living with me, not even Lenny. We get along for 24 hours and that's that. In 1999 when I was living on the East Side of town I gave a talent show. Ma and my female friend Laura, we gave out gifts to everyone in the room. There were around 28 people present. It was a big sunny room with big windows. You could see the grass and trees. I cooked a turkey and made two apple pies. I wanted everyone to get up and sing or say something about yourself. Ma and I sang a song "Motel Made For Love." I was dancing to the '70s music. There were another mother and son who got up to sing. We all had a good time. My cousin G-G came over to join in the party.

> **FLASHBACK:** 2001 September 8th I gave myself a birthday party. People brought food to join in. we danced. My feet are not so good now, going back to 1999.

I was in a play with the Hansberry Sands Theater here in Milwaukee on the East Side. The play was Black Nativity. It was nice, just too cold for me.

Guess what?! I got paid! Party! Party! Well, no joke! I got paid! I was sick, but I got paid! The sun is shining on me, thank you Lord! After my birthday party on September 8th, then 9/11, those two planes flew into the World Trade Center towers. It was a sad day all over this world.

Again in 1999 I had an audition downtown for a movie called Elevator. I didn't make the cut. That same year I went down to Illinois to audition for this modeling company. I payed $100 for one night in a hotel down there and spent $250 there to walk up and down in front of those people who were looking for all kinds of looks and sizes. It was a lot of money that I spent down there, but I thought I'm worth it. I auditioned for the movie Book of Numbers in Harlem at the YMCA on 135th Street. I wanted to audition for the movie Sparkle, but I needed an agent, which I didn't have.

I have messed up part of my life, drinking and getting high. It's 2001. I always catch a cold in winter.

My mother and I flew to New York on August 5th, 2001, the summer before, to attend a party for our great aunt. She would be 90 years old. The day we left it was really hot in Milwaukee and in New York when we got there. Ma went to her friend Ruby's place in the Bronx. She had air conditioning there. I stayed at Wendell's house on the other side of the Bronx.

When we got to the party aunt Lil's three daughters were there, Reno, Ron, and Reba, and Carmen and her two children were present. My aunt can pass for 70 or 75, she looks so young. Lenny was there too. We were having a good time, good food, and good dancing. The music wasn't all that, but we danced anyway.

So around 10 PM ma was ready to go. Her portable oxygen was low. We said good night and caught a cab to Ruby's place. I took ma up there. Then Wendell called to pick me up to go to his place, so I kissed ma good night and left.

For that week ma wasn't feeling well. The day we left it was hard to call a cab to the airport, but we finally got one. Off we went back to Milwaukee a week later. It was still hot.

If I could talk about my grandfather a little, I found out that gramps had saved a letter from 1944 telling gramps it was from the Providence Defense Recreation Committee in Rhode Island, thanking him for providing real high class entertainment for the servicemen on leave. Gramps used to live down the street from the Clinton Rose Center. What I found out about him was that gramps liked to wine and dine everybody. I have the same ways. I wanted people to be happy, to have a good time when I was on the scene. That we both performed at the Apollo Theater, he in 1946 and '48, and me in 1988, we also had in common.

Before we left Wendell and I went downtown around the World Trade Center to buy a few things to bring back to Milwaukee. When we made it to ma's house in Milwaukee my bag broke just when I put our bags down. There's an old saying, Time flies when you are having fun. That's true. Anyway, once ma settled in I called myself a cab to go to my apartment, which was on the East Side of town.

I was thinking about how ma and Auntie had been coming to Milwaukee since the early '50s. Milwaukee is where they made beer and cheese. And gramps made it his home. I'm glad that my grandfather settled here in the Midwest. It's not Harlem or Brooklyn or the Bronx. So when I came to Milwaukee I brought a little bit of Harlem, Brooklyn and the Bronx with me.

In other words, I took Milwaukee by storm in early 1991 and '92. I always liked to sing. I could sing pop music, R and B, and jazz, as I have said. I'm what you could call an all around performer, singer, dancer and actor. Wherever there is an audition, I'm there. And so to you the Reader, I did make it in New York my way.

Why can't I be happy for once? My relationship is out the window. I'm not good with love on a one on one thing basis. I never was. That's what been missing in my life. I must say that there is a mystery about me. Sometimes when I wake up in the morning I wonder who is Lucky going to be today? I said once that this is a Show Tune, but the show hasn't been written yet. I think Lucky just didn't grow up with his voice and looks. After all, I am a lucky man.

FLASHBACK: Now it is 2002, cold...just plain cold! Ma wasn't feeling too well, so I decided to stick around. Ma was in the hospital while I was in a musical. Ma was real sick. We did four weekend shows and five shows in two days. No time to think...just do it. The play was recorded on tape so I took the camcorder. She laughed when she saw me in it. I was running between checking on ma's apartment, going by my place, take a shower, back to the hospital, then back to the theater to do my thing.

FLASHBACK: Ma came home at the end of February. I stayed over at her apartment more often. I got me some butter cookies and ma some ice cream. I wanted very much to help her in any way that I could. Ma had by now a home attended, or home nurse, who had come to love her like a daughter. I could see that sometimes when Becky would take her out to the store she would have her son's car or his truck. I got ma Meals On Wheels now. So I got used to eating with ma when she would eat. Sometimes I would bring in some pancakes and juice for her and my-self. My sister brought her some food also.

FLASHBACK: I flew to New York now, just to take a break. I was only there for a week, but saw my family, my great aunt Lil in the Bronx, stopped down in Harlem where I always went to see my and ma's best friend Rita and Sam on 114th Street. Then I went down to Central Park West to see some friends.

FLASHBACK: I got back home to Milwaukee. It's early March. I called ma, but no one answered. I called the desk, they have a key, so people went up to her apartment door. There was no answer. I was holding on damn long now. She couldn't answer her phone or her door. I put the phone down. I wasn't even dressed, but I called a cab. I had my long raincoat on. I found them working on ma. They took ma to the hospital. I rode with her. Where she was living I couldn't get a test.

FLASHBACK: So now ma was back in the hospital again. I called my sister Lucy to come over and I called g-G. They both came to the hospital. Ma was having some breathing trouble with her lungs. She returned home after five days. Then I said to ma, "Ma, I'd love to get you out of here."

There was a lady who worked in an office where I lived. She was already a friend of ma's. You would have thought that they had been friends for 20 or 30 years. Anyway, she said, yes, and I got an appointment to bring ma here. I was now living in a high rise apartment building on the 17th floor. My mother got an apartment on the third floor. It was real good this way. I could be close to her at any time.

FLASHBACK: Yes, I was happy that she was there. I would still go down there and spent the night. Ma was getting two meals a day, from Meals On Wheels. Her home attended started coming over to take her to the store somewhere. One time I was outside the building in the parking lot when they came back. When ma came out she almost fell, so I told Becky not to take ma out any more, because if she did fall Becky would get into a lot of trouble. I told ma that I would go to the store for her and get her anything that she wanted. A friend of my mother's came over to see her and made her smile. She was ma's friend, not mine. And my sister came to visit her. I could see in ma's eyes that she loved her.

I would tape ma when she was feeling okay and was still going with her to the doctor's office. Ma found out that she had cancer and it might be moving up into her head. There was a special test that the doctor wanted her to have. My sister asked me, "Did she want to have that test?" She said she didn't know. So we prayed for ma out loud, hoping that God would hear, I prayed to keep her here with me.

Well, ma's health was going downhill. She cried all of the time now. I didn't know what to do or what to say. She said to me, "Lucky, I feel like throwing myself into the river" which was down the hill on the way to the supermarket. I got upset. Who would I talk to now. I forgot to call my priest, but I didn't want to leave ma alone, now and forever. I know God has plans for all of us.

As I said before, I was taping ma when she was eating or watching TV in her chair. I tried to make her laugh. Ma would stop crying for awhile. Her next appointment was September 22nd, 2002. It was coming up to my birthday September 12th. I put on my white suit and hat, and ma gave me $100 for my birthday. I gave her a kiss on the forehead. I told ma that I would be back in a few hours. I went to gamble and lost all of ma's money. So I came back and told ma that I had lost all of my money. I was still trying to make ma smile, but I could see that she wasn't feeling well at all.

I called New York. They told me that my great aunt Lil was in the hospital there in the Bronx.

On September 23rd in the morning ma got up to eat something, got dressed and the van came around 10 AM. We got to her doctor's office. She had to wait. Ma had to lay her head on my lap. She was sick. I think ma just wanted the pain to go away. When the doctor called us inside he could see that ma was sick. He asked someone there to drive the two of us to the hospital. When we got there they took us up to the fourth floor.

This is hard for me to live through all over again. Anything that I said before, I will not take back, not for anyone in the world, but I would have died for my mother and Auntie. My God knows what I did for my mother, my Auntie, my father, uncle and cousins. If I had to do it all over again I would do the same thing, maybe more. I didn't know that ma wanted that test. I could tell you how strong love is. Love is very strong, if it's used in a good way. I love my two mothers to death.

When I first got to Milwaukee my grandfather was living on the North Side of town. I don't remember the street. It was off 3rd Streets. Then about a year later ma and my sister moved gramps over to Wells Street. He would be closer to ma and me. Around a month later someone called ma and said they saw gramps walking with two young ladies on Wisconsin Avenue. Gramps was in his 80s by now.

Back to me. She went ahead and had the test done. I didn't know what to think. Yes, I was so worried. Well I waited until they brought her back. She had blood on her top lip. She smiled at me. I knew that she was in pain. I thought, Why her? They took ma upstairs to the fifth floor, the hospice floor. The doctor said that she would be there just one day and then they would take her back down stairs to her room on the lower floor. I said, Okay.

Meanwhile in came Ge-Ge. I guess she called my sister. Ge-Ge came by that evening. Ma was sitting up. She told Ge-Ge, "You know I'm not going to be here long." It was September 30th, 2002 at 1:45 PM. I was leaving. I said that I was going home to take a shower. I'd be right back.

I came back around an hour later and brought my camera. I had gotten some film, and ma's hat and scarf. I asked the nurse to take six or so pictures of ma and me. Ma said, Hello. I put her hat on her while she was eating apple sauce and cream of wheat. On September 30th I got back to my apartment. It was Tuesday when she went into a deep sleep.

By this time my sister and her daughter came into her room. We did not speak to each other. I called Wendell in the Bronx. He wanted to come here, so I paid his airline tickets, for him and for his son. Before I left the room the doctor told me they gave ma 5-7 days to live. I lost it in my heart and soul. I almost couldn't speak. I called ma's best friend Ruby and told her what the doctor had told me. She said she was coming by train. This was right before Wendell got here.

My sister and play sister were sitting in the back by the wall at the foot of her bed. I went downstairs to get a soda and came right back. It had been two days since ma went into her coma. When I got to the doorway I called her name, "Mae? Mae Kept?" My mother sat up in her bed and looked at me halfway to the left for maybe three seconds. I was the last person she laid eyes on. I was happy and sad.

> FLASHBACK: Let me say this again, when I went down to get a soda I came right back. My sister and play sister were sitting by the wall. I called ma's name in the doorway, "Mae? Mae Kept?" Don't you know my mother sat straight up in her bed, turned half way to the left where I was standing and looked at me for three seconds, her eye blank. I could not believe it! I was the last person she saw. I cried out loud and I was happy at the same time.

> FLASHBACK: I could not leap over to ma to hold her up long enough, but I called out loud, "God please! Please take one of my limbs!" I didn't care who was in the room. I think Wendell and his son came the next day. So now almost everybody was there, but Ruby. She was on her way now. I could not stop crying. I called my daughter. It was October 2nd. I Told her what was going on. All she talked about was her daughter's birthday was coming up and she would try to call my son who was in the army. He went into the army right after high school

> FLASHBACK: It is Sunday, October 5th. Someone else picked Ruby up at the train station. They brought her right to the hospital. Ruby thought that ma would wake up. I told her, no. Then I told her what the doctor had told me. She started crying then. So then I left to go home and clean up.

> FLASHBACK: My heart was feeling heavy. I hoped my heart wouldn't break. But, what the hell, my mother was 72 years old now.

While I was at home I called back to ma's room. Ruby said that everybody was taking over mother's room! I said that I would be right there. I got dressed, called a cab, and got over there, telling everyone to, "Get the hell out of my mother's room!" I said, "And I don't care who you are!" My play sister came over to ask what was wrong? I said, "There's' too many people here in mother's room. They could go in the other room and watch TV, and sit on soft chairs in there!" Well, some of them left and went home.

> **FLASHBACK:** I was rubbing ma's arm, wiping her face. I told whoever was in the room to "Touch her. Let her know you. She can still hear you." The hearing is the last thing to go the doctor had said. I almost fell apart. It's not time to give up Lucky, I said to myself. I gave my sister the information at the nurses' station.

> **FLASHBACK:** After Ruby came I left so Ruby would have some time by herself with ma to talk to her. Now it was October 8th in the morning. I spent the night there. I told Ruby I would be back. I went home for a few. It was around 4 PM or 4:30 when I got up. I called a cab and arrived about 4:55 PM. My sister and her daughter were there, Wendell and his son also. Ge-Ge was there. I started to walk out of the room when Ruby said out loud, "She stopped breathing." I know my mother heard me leaving. I think she was waiting for me to get back, so she started to breathe again. I returned. The next moment she stopped breathing for good.

The doctor came in and timed the death for the death certificate. It was 5 PM October 8th, 2002 that my mother's life stopped right in front of me. I was crying, crying like Ruby and Wendell and Ge-Ge and my sister and her daughter. I said The Lord's Prayer. I fell to my knees on the floor. I cried and I cried. I cried out loud and you know, ma's soul left her body. You see, I didn't know until now that love is good, love is powerful. I could not stop. Ma had a little smile on her face as if to say, Son I'm free of pain now. Son I'm with the Lord. I could not believe it.

FLASHBACK: So, for some reason ma let me know that it was okay. I think my mother up above was looking down on me, seeing how hard I was crying. I was crying. I was down on the floor. I didn't want anybody to say anything to me today. All I could think of was, What else can happen? I wanted so much to end my life. It seems the right thing to do, but I tried to stay strong. I told the people who worked in my building what happened. They gave me a hug.

FLASHBACK: While we were still in ma's room, before we could get her things together, two attendants came into her room with a stretcher and a black bag. They just picked her up and put her inside that black bag. I thought I was going insane or something. I cried out loud...real loud. I was going to follow her down the hall. I stopped.

We got her things together in a few bags. I called my daughter to tell her what had happened. All she said was about her daughter's birthday which was in October also. This was October 8th 5 PM, 2002. I was numb in my heart and in my head. I called my doctor to tell him what happened, to send me some sleeping pills. I think I was used these words most often: my sister and I would make the funeral arrangements. My heart felt very heavy.

Two days later we had the viewing. Wendell was still in Milwaukee, but he had to leave with his son. In the meantime I had made an appointment a year before that I had to keep. It fell on the same day as ma's viewing. So I left in a cab headed for the V.A. They waited for me. I got through the test and headed back to the funeral home to be there. No one was there.

Ma's funeral was the next day, Friday October 11th 2002. It was sad how some people can be cold as ice from top to bottom.

FLASHBACK: It was time for my mother's funeral at

Northwest Chapel. Thinking back when I was little, when my mother took me up to the roof of the White Hall hotel, it was 11 stories high. She was going to throw me and her off the roof. .

The funeral started and I asked one of my cousins to go to s to get some film. When he returned I found that he had gotten the wrong film. Well, that's that.

I said I wanted ma's casket open, but my sister said she wanted it closed. So we were at odds with one another. She wanted it closed, I wanted it open. My mother looked like a queen.

So then my sister's husband said, "Don't talk to my wife like that!"

I turned around to look at him. He was standing right behind me. He said to me, "Turn around! Don't look at me! I will see you outside after the funeral."

Well, just that second I looked at my mother, who I know said in my heart, Lucky don't do it. Meanwhile my sister told him to leave it alone. All I could think about was how my grandmother's life was taken before I was born. Ma came here to build a bridge with her own daughter.

They pushed her into another room where I gave her a kiss, took pictures and video of her in the casket, and said to her, "I'll be seeing you soon, ma."

FLASHBACK: Ruby was here for three weeks. They all said that I was mean to her. I know I didn't mean to. Until this day I just know that I was going to die from a broken heart. My doctor knew how close I was to my mother and gave me some sleeping pills to help me to sleep. Sometimes it worked, sometimes it didn't. So I just went with the flow, you dig? I know one thing: I know people were talking about me behind my back. As long an they don't put their hands on me, got it Jack?

So now I had to go and clean my mother's apartment. I sold her bed to someone in the building. I gave the two drser drawers to my cousin for his family. I gave the TV to Ge-Ge. I found someone in the building to buy the tape player that I gave her and her little glass table set I sold. I did get all of mother's papers out of there and took them to my place. Some of the women in the building came in to go through her clothes and she had two sports jackets that I bought her the year before for her birthday. They were green and red. Ma liked color. Her air conditioner I took to my place, and her 12" TV too. There was a futon couch that I gave to one of my cousins. I took my mother's couch up to my place. It opened to a queen size bed.

I know my other cousins told my great aunt Lil, who was still in the hospital, of ma's death. She cried and cried like a baby. You see that was her sister's daughter. And I called down to Central Park West where we both have friends that are like family. One guy, his family is from New York. They are like my own family. I think that they felt the pain as I did. You see, I had made friends with them, their mother and father. They still send me cards on Christmas. That always helps the healing.

> FLASHBACK: When JFK Jr.'s plane was missing off the coast of Long Island and they later found the bodies I sent a sympathy card. Well, don't you know, I got a reply from the Kennedy family. I keep the card in my picture album. That makes me a human being.

> FLASHBACK: Let me bring things up to speed. On the first anniversary of my mother's passing I held a memorial fund raiser dinner where I lived. I thought I was going to take a long trip, but then thought, no. So, I made up some fliers with ma's picture in the middle, saying this money would be for treatment of cancer and research for the American Cancer Society. It was held on May 3d. I sent out fliers all over down south in New York.

I raised $100 from the event down south, and I got another $100 from aunt Lil from the Bronx. And in my building I raised $134 and change that made me feel pretty good. I sang three songs. I cried and I laughed, even told a few jokes. I cooked again. I made two cakes, coffee and tea.

> **FLASHBACK**: You know sometimes one person's can make a difference. All you need is good idea and go for it, right?

> **FLASHBACK**: I put in $400 of my own into the fund raiser, altogether it made $740 for the American Cancer Society. I sent the check in my mother's name.

A few months later, in 2002 while I was sleeping, someone touched my upper back, right below my neck. I knew it was ma who touched me. And about a week later someone lightly slapped my outer thigh. It was either ma or Auntie. I called my aunt Lil in New York, to tell her about it, and I called Ruby to tell her what happened. I know love is a strong tool: they can let me know that they are watching over me. They are my angels, always with me. I do believe in the after life, that your loved ones can come back and either touch you or brush up near your bed, or chair.

So now it's December 2003. this time of the year I was feeling kind of sad. As I was talking about my grandfather, where he was living on Wells Street, he was about five blocks from me. My sister got a call that some woman was taking gramps' checks and maybe taking his money.

When I walked over there my sister had her little gun in one hand and her bible in the other hand saying, she was going to shoot the first woman walking down the stairs! I calmed her down. After that ma and my sister were looking for another place for him. They found a group home for gramps, more of a nursing home. It was a nice place that was run by family members. Within a month we moved gramps in there. He seemed to like it there.

Going back, my mother told me when she was 16 and Auntie was 15, gramps introduced them to Ms Billy Holiday and Nat King Cole at the Apollo, going up to his dressing room. My mother and Auntie were trying to catch a cab on Broadway around 3 or 4 AM in the morning. Ma shared a cab with Burt Lancaster. The cab driver thought he was going to get a big tip, but Mr. Burt gave my mother his share of the fare.

Let me go on about my grandfather. I came across some pictures of gramps taking in the 50s from Long Beach, California where he played the piano and sang. There were pictures of him inn Oakland, California as well. I found out that the family picture and the story about my grandfather had been in the Milwaukee Journal. Auntie was here visiting. My grandfather was born in Mount Vernon, New York. My mother and Auntie were also born there. My grandfather played mostly all over Wisconsin. He worked with Ms Ella Fitzgerald, and others. He played in South Bend, Indiana; Montana; Kenosha, Racine, Eau Clair, and Martinique, Wisconsin; and San Fransisco. I'm very proud of my grandfather and he never learned how to read music or write it. And let's not leave out Green Bay, Wisconsin.

Now my grandfather had settled into his new place. There they could feed themselves, and watch TV. I left my keyboard there for him to play. I know it's good for the fingers, I'm told. That was my keyboard that I had brought with me from New York City.

I have to say that life throws you a curve ball. In my mother's case there were a lot of them, but she caught all of them and started being a working class person of New York City. My mother got knocked down and got right back up. I got knocked down and got right back up. That one part of my life I'll always remember until the day I die.

Part of my life was good, some happy: my first kiss with my first girlfriend on Fox Street, the Bronx. In 1963 I once thought the whole world is a stage and everybody is playing their part. If there is one thing that I learned it is that I never do unto others as they do unto me. Where would it lead? No where, right? If I could count the auditions that I have gone to it would be around 35-45, both here and in New York.

So it is now 2007, the winter month of March. I will never

forget where I came from. I'm just telling it like it is. Sometimes I have to step back, that means just to see what I look like, what's in my brain, my heart and soul? If I like what I see, then I could continue to be me. That's the confidence that I have. I think I build up my confidence around five or six years of age. Oh well. As I said before, I feel great and I look great for me to be going on 59 years of age. So until we meet again, this story has refreshed my mind and body. Did my story do anything for you, my Reader? I guess I'm no better than anyone else.

After my mother passed away I didn't know if I was going to stay in Milwaukee or what. Well, here I won't be too far from that part of my family that came here from New York. I know my mother and Auntie are proud of me anyway. Now it is 2007. I feel great and look great. My grandmother's sister is still in New York, the Bronx. She is 95 going on 96. I always go to see her when I'm in New York. All of my studies are fine tuning my craft.

In 1993 in Milwaukee we were all happy. My singing teacher back in New York and my piano teacher from Harlem told me never let anyone step on your dream. In today's world you have to be ready for anything that comes at you and you could take that to the bank, Lucky.

> **FLASHBACK:** Going back to the early 70s in south Bronx, Auntie and Uncle Freddy had an apartment on Hoe Avenue. Well, from what I can remember, Uncle Freddy was arguing about something and I think Uncle was going to hit Auntie. My first cousin Lenny pulled his knife out and put it to Uncle Freddy's throat, cutting it. Then Lenny got scared. He went to my father's place in Brooklyn where Loni had an attic apartment. Now Uncle got to the hospital in time. He did not file charges against Lenny.

So things happen so fast. I had a 22 gun on me. Now Wendell heard what happened to his father. Wendell hit my mother in the face. He said, he did not know why.

I still remind him that anyone that puts their hands on my

mother will pay for that and Wendell does not know when I am going to do that to him. He knows about it, because I told the whole family. I mean the ones that care. There are those in the family who do not care and I could not care for them. Remember, God knows what went wrong. Anybody that did my mother wrong will pay for it, whether here in Milwaukee or in New York City. In God's house there is justice. Everyone goes through that. Anyway, when my father told Lenny to go to Milwaukee and lay low for awhile, this was around 1973.

*O*n a lighter note, my cousin Carmen was giving herself a 50th birthday party down in Savanna, Georgia. Her birthday was February 10th. I, Ge-Ge, and April and her mother Cookie flew down there on her birthday. It was a Saturday. April got us rooms right next to each other, and two single beds. The rooms were nice. I had to be quiet. April rented a car. That was cool, being with three women going shopping for the party. We all chipped in to buy Carmen a nice CD. The party was to be in black and white, or all white or all black.

We got to our rooms around 3 PM, when the party was over. I lay down for awhile. We went to get something to eat. All I know is that it was chicken, fries and soda. At around 5:30 AM we started getting dressed. I shared a room with Ge-Ge as we always got along.

Driving to find the party it had been getting dark. So we were driving all around. It was 7 PM. I said, "We're late you guys." When we walked in there were only a few people there. So I said out loud, "We're from Milwaukee!" They told us that Carmen wanted to wait until more people same in. So I went to their cash bar for three rum and cokes, and wine for me.

People started coming in about an hour later. Carmen's two sons were there. There was a red carpet for her to walk down as she came in. the D.J. Announced her as she came in. There were red roses on each side of the carpet. The D.J. Also announced her two sons' arrival and her two brothers'. Before you knew it there was a full house. My cousin looked like a movie star, with this bad red dress on and a brown stole.

I started feeling the wine. All the music was from the '70s. I sang a song called "If You Look Into Your Heart" from the movie Sparkle. I danced. I felt like I was 25 or 30 years old again.

Then I took pictures of the birthday girl and all of us. The food was really good. There were three cakes. It was something to never forget. I was around Carmen for 48 years. We came along way. My hat of to you Carmen.

The party started getting really hot on the dance floor. I didn't know that I could dance that long. They started doing the Bus Stop. I was very proud of Carmen. She worked her way up...with the help of her girlfriend who put the party all together. And Carmen, she does not smoke or drink. She was the last one still dancing. They told us there was an After Set at one of Carmen's girlfriend's house. I din't go. Someone took me back to my room. It was around 11 PM.

You should have seen my cousin Ge-Ge. That rum really got her in a good mood, she was dancing by herself. And a guy with a dark hat on was up on Carmen. I told Ge-Ge to turn around and see who was dancing behind her. We all took family pictures. I just miss Carmen's young son David.

I forgot to tell you which hotel we stayed in. It was the Holiday Inn. We only stayed until Monday. April had to take a car back. Wouldn't you know it, all of us just talked until around 7:30 AM when Carmen came to April's room. She had brought eggs and grits, coffee and juice. That's what it's all about: family. Our family had gotten small, here in Milwaukee and New York.

FLASHBACK: There was another time Ge-Ge went to New

York by herself. My family was having a cookout. When they have one it's a big, big cookout. Ge-Ge said she had a nice time there. Lenny and his wife came down to the city and took Ge-Ge Upstate to Newburg. It was 60 miles up river. I think she stayed a week. Carmen had a seven month old grandson. Before we left we stopped over to Carmen's house. We saw Carmen's daughter and her two kids, a daughter around five or six, the son about six months old. I asked the mother. I held the little one. He was small, but solid and I got a smile too. I'm going to buy him a drum set when he gets two years old, I thought.

FLASHBACK: Sorry to leave you hanging in the story like that. Between 2003 and the present I moved three times, flew to New York city and down to Georgia. I think I move so often because I don't let the grass grow under my feet. I've just been taking care of myself.

FLASHBACK: In the mid '80s m father went to jail. He almost killed someone in his apartment. I went to court for him. The judge told him, "Is it true Mr. Kept, that you took a knife and put it in the guy's chest?" He answered, "Yes." The judge gave my father nine months in jail years probation.

Love is writing on my paper
Love can also be the passion of my dance
Love and music goes together
Remember one world, one son, one moon
Love is poetry of my own
Remember God loves you no matter what
This has been a journey and a blast
Thank you and good night.

Summer Time

In the breeze of the summer night
I'll go on and hold you tight.
And in the afternoon, when the sky is blue
That's when I'll be thinking of you.
In the early morning dawn, I'll whisper I love you
And we'll play on the lawn
And the grass is green and still wet
'Cause you look your best.
In the Summer time we'll walk by the beach and hold hands
'Cause I know our love has no demands.
Later in the day, while we're apart
Your love beats on deeper in the heart.
That's why I say, In the breeze of the Summer night
When every thing's asleep, I'll hold you tight.
Hold me sweats, yeah right here come on closer
There's nothing to fear, with you and I they all can see the love
We share will always be in the Summer time.

February 20th, 1976

Once In A Life Time

Once in a life time as the nights go by.
It was the beginning of my end.
I sat and sat and nothing happened.
Although my mind was still, I can still hear the whisper.
Once in a life time, I can feel ten feet tall.
I'm looking down on everybody.
In my thoughts felt unknown, Unknown to the days of my life.
Once I felt so happy, So happy that I started to cry.
I listened to the sound of the wind.
As the leaves fell to the ground, They seem to form a word.
The same word the wind sent into my ear.
I looked oh how I love thee blue of you.
The tenderness we both feel, Arms reaching out.
As the sun and the moon came together.
Once in a life time, I can feel myself getting high.
Now I'M high as the stars above.
I see in my high happy lovers in each others arms.
I thought I wish that was me.
In my high it was soft like a kitten.
Again I reached out.
And when I did that, All my once in a life time was over.

November 1971

Printed in the United States
by Baker & Taylor Publisher Services